THE JERSEY LILY

MRS. LANGTRY

The
JERSEY
LILY

The Life & Times
of Lillie Langtry

Sonia Hillsdon

SEAFLOWER BOOKS

First published in 1993
New edition 1996; Reprinted 1998

SEAFLOWER BOOKS
Seaflower Books is an imprint of
EX LIBRIS PRESS
1 The Shambles
Bradford on Avon
Wiltshire
BA15 1JS

Typeset in 10 point Century Schoolbook

Design and typesetting by Ex Libris Press
Cover printed by Shires Press, Trowbridge, Wiltshire
Printed and bound in Great Britain by
Cromwell Press Ltd., Trowbridge, Wiltshire

ISBN 0 948578 55 6

*With grateful thanks to the following
for their help and encouragement:*
Cienne Jurd, Jersey Library; Jonathan Carter, Jersey
Museum; Betty Bois, St. Saviour; Monty Doong, St. Helier

Acknowledgements: To Jersey Museum, Jersey Library and Jersey
Tourism for loan of illustrations and to the Société Jersiaise for help
in their reproduction.

CONTENTS

Foreword

Lillie Langtry's fearless attitude to life and her remarkable achievements make her sound like one of today's liberated women. So the extracts used in this book from her autobiography and other publications of the period serve as a constant reminder that we are reading about an energetic, fun-loving woman who was born nearly a hundred and fifty years ago. As we follow her story through good times and bad we can also imagine her responding to both experiences with her favourite retort, 'Don't let's fuss, please.'

Sonia Hillsdon, Jersey

About the Author

Sonia Hillsdon is an English graduate who, after enjoying full-time teaching of her subject for many years, now combines it part-time with writing. Her interest in the past was stimulated by her move to Jersey over twenty years ago and she has been grateful for the many opportunities given her to share her research into the Island's history with a wider public. She was, therefore, delighted to be asked to write this short biography of Lillie Langtry, as this nineteenth century Jersey woman has always appeared to her to be made up of such fascinating contradictions.

Sonia Hillsdon is also the author of the following books:

Jersey Witches, Ghosts and Traditions, 1984.

Jersey Occupation Remembered, 1986.

Strange Stories from Jersey, 1987.

A Taste of Jersey, 1987.

The Visitor's Guide to Jersey, 1988.

A series of 10 local history books for children, 1994-6.

IMPORTANT DATES

1853	Lillie born St. Saviour's Rectory, 13th October	
1874	Married Edward Langtry at St. Saviour's Church	Aged 20
1877	Introduced to Prince of Wales	Aged 23
1878	Presented to Queen Victoria	Aged 24
1880	Met Prince Louis of Battenberg	Aged 26
1881	Birth of Jeanne-Marie/ First appearance on London Stage	Aged 27
1882	First American stage tour	Aged 29
1887	Became American citizen; divorced Edward Langtry	Aged 33
1891	Appeared Theatre Royal, Jersey	Aged 37
1897	Won Cesarewitch with own horse 'Merman'	Aged 44
1900	Opened Opera House, Jersey	Aged 46
1901	Bought Imperial Theatre, London	Aged 47
1906	First appearance Vaudeville	Aged 52
1907	Broke the bank at Monte Carlo	Aged 53
1909	Wrote novel All at Sea	Aged 55
1913	Appeared in silent film	Aged 60
1925	Wrote autobiography	Aged 72
1929	Died in Monaco; buried at St. Saviour's Church	Aged 75

Sir Thomas Le Breton Senior (1763-1838) Bailiff

William Le Breton = Jane Hue

William Corbet Le Breton (1815-88) = Emilie Davis Martin (1821-1902)
Dean of Jersey (1850-88)

Sir Thomas Le Breton Jr.
(1791-1857)
Bailiff (1848-57)

Francis
(1843-1872)
Bengal Pilot Service
d. Calcutta

William
(1846-1924)
Indian Staff Corps
= Elizabeth Price (1873)

Trevor-Alexander
(1847-1870)
Royal Marine Light Infantry
d. Toronto

Maurice
(1849-1881)

Reginald
(1855-1876)

Clement-Martin
(1851-1927)
Barrister at Law
K.C. 1904
= Alice Jones, daughter
of Lord Ranelagh

Emilie Charlotte (Lillie)
(1853-1929)

= 1.   (1874) Edward Langtry
        d. Chester 1897

= 2.   (1899) Hugo, eldest
        son of Sir Hugo de Bathe (Bart)
        (1874-1940)

1 A Daughter for the Dean of Jersey

BORN BEAUTIFUL, WITH COURAGE AND intelligence to match, what exactly were the circumstances of Lillie Langtry's birth and upbringing which enabled her to take every advantage of these natural assets? What kind of world was this most famous woman of her time born into, nearly a century and a half ago?

In Jersey, her birthplace, in October 1853, the year of her birth, *La Chronique de Jersey* reported turbulent times both abroad and in the island: 'Toute l'attention de notre population se divise en ce moment entre la grande question russo-turque, la marche du choléra, et la cherté des substances alimentaires.'

For non-French speaking newcomers to this largest of the Channel Islands, the *Jersey Times* covered all these concerns in English. Its European column announced, 'After extraordinary patience and forbearance the Sultan (of Turkey) has declared war against Russia.' It carried, too, the important news of the urgent anti-cholera campaign in St. Helier, the Island's capital. On the food front it told its readers, 'For shipping or for freight as also for cattle, sheep, corn and all kinds of agricultural produce the prices are enormous.' Another headline, 'The Dear Times and the Bad Weather' seemed to say it all.

The equinoctial gales that October were causing havoc to shipping between England and the Channel Islands, with Jersey so dependent on the regular shipment of goods and mail in and out of the Island. This 'boisterous weather' also caused concern for the then just launched, 1,800 ton *Matilda Wallenbach* – the largest ship ever built in Jersey.

Less life-threatening items also featured in both papers that month. In an Island noted for its ready recourse to the law, there was great interest in the case of Jersey's Attorney-General v. John Le Couteur who, in his position as a Colonel in the Royal Jersey Militia, was accused of certain alleged expressions libellous and detrimental to the character, honour and dignity of the Bailiff, Sir Thomas Le Breton, the civil head of the Island.

The 'ungenial character of the season' also affected one of the many classes in the Island's important Royal Jersey Agricultural and Horticultural Society Autumn Show – the *Jersey Times* reporter finding very little to admire in the indifferent supply of flowers and plants in the horticultural section.

However, in the report of the dinner that followed that Autumn Show on Wednesday, 12th October, the *Jersey Times* had an incidental detail that, in fact, had a direct reference to the Dean of Jersey and his only daughter. At the dinner the Chairman explained to the guests that 'The Dean had intended that day to dine with the Society but that domestic circumstances had unfortunately prevented him.' Indeed, the Dean of Jersey, the Very Rev. William Corbet Le Breton, and his wife Emilie Davis (née Martin) were daily expecting the arrival of their sixth child.

The very next day, Thursday 13th October, 1853, in this unique Channel Island garrisoned against France by British and Jersey regiments; where a Bailiff was chief Magistrate and States President; where French was spoken by the majority of the 57,000 inhabitants; where agriculture, fishing and shipbuilding were the main sources of income, Emilie Charlotte was born. A daughter for Jersey's Dean; a sister for five brothers; a girl with a gloriously free childhood ahead of her; a woman who would live through another war with Turkey and Russia on opposing sides; a peerless beauty whose fame would spread far beyond the small island of her birth and whose charisma would attract many men to her side including the Prince of Wales, the future Edward VII.

Coincidentally, the same day that Emilie Le Breton was born, the twelve-year-old Prince of Wales was travelling down by train from Balmoral – where the Royal Family had been holidaying – with Queen Victoria, Prince Albert and their other children, back to Windsor Castle.

Emilie was born at home, in the Rectory of St. Saviour's Church, where her father held the position of both Rector and Dean, the latter a Crown appointment that also made him head of the Anglican Church in Jersey. In her autobiography, *The Days I Knew*, written when she was over seventy, she remembered the Rectory, or Deanery as it was called during her father's incumbency, in great detail, it 'snuggled comfortably at the bottom of a hilly lane leading from the parish main road. It was built of the grey granite quarried in the Island, and occupied three sides of a square; two sides were covered by the dwelling; the third, forming the large courtyard, being given over to a row of buildings used in olden days for the home-manufacture of cider. The making of this mild beverage had long been discontinued but the great stone wheel for the crushing of the apples together with the huge stone troughs, vats, and other primitive appliances still remained, while a dove-cote, symbolical of the rector's calling, stood in the courtyard.

A portion of the house proper bore the date of 1100, cut in a coping stone, but the original building had evidently been added to from time to time. Its face was almost entirely covered with climbing roses – red, white, blush and (to me, the most beautiful of all) the single damask. Underlying these were cherry and pear trees of great age, the blossoms of which in springtime mingled with the roses in delicious disorder. Climbing to my own bedroom window, and gracefully framing it, was an immense white jessamine warring for existence with a vigorous climbing deep-red rose.

The large, high-walled garden to the east was given equally to flowers and fruit, and here a fig tree – rich, in season, with its purple yield – reared its fertile head. To the south, a long terrace with a gently sloping lawn beyond comprised the remainder of the pleasure grounds, with evidence on all sides of my mother's wonderful love of flowers. There was also a large portion of the glebe fields stocked with vegetables to satisfy our healthy appetites, and which at times we all helped to weed.

The Old Rectory, St. Saviour

There were two main entrances to the rectory, the door consecrated to my mother's use being dignified with a glass portico, always well filled with flowering plants in sharp contrast to the severely, business-like entrance to my father's study and our schoolroom. The first floor was a labyrinth of small, low rooms, with deep window-seats and many-paned casements; these rooms were divided into groups approached by separate and winding stairs. A drawing-room and dining-room, which had been added by my father, seemed almost palatial in comparison with the rest of the house.

Looking out on the slanting lawn at the rear, these rooms commanded a view of the beautiful undulating lands that are known in Jersey as "côtils".'

~

Almost immediately, perhaps because of the extreme whiteness of her skin, the baby Emilie was nicknamed 'Lillie' by her family. It was a name which stayed with her for the rest of her life and which she much preferred to either Emilie or Charlotte – 'both dreadful to my way of thinking.'

Also strongly emphasised in her autobiography is the fact that the Le Breton family, into which she had been born, was a distinguished Jersey family. For instance, Sir Thomas Le Breton, the Bailiff about whom John Le Couteur was alleged to have made disparaging remarks, was her great-uncle. Even after the celebrity she became in her own right as Lillie Langtry, she was still proud to recall: 'My remote ancestors were seigneurs of Noirmont, a very picturesquely situated manor on the seashore, and one of them was among the Jerseymen who followed William the Conqueror and fought in the Battle of Hastings. He figures in the Bayeux tapestry and this fact incited me recently to inspect the famous fabric for the purpose of tracing in the features of this distinguished person a resemblance to myself, but the results were not very satisfactory. He also seems to have had some dispute regarding the boundary of the seigneurie, and took his grievance to Rouen, Normandy, where the facts were chronicled in the archives of that ancient city.

Another Le Breton was a bishop under Edward I and, in the same King's reign, the family contributed a Judge Le Breton who seems to have run through his money and to have become so hard-up that the King graciously presented him with his robes. I only hope he served His Majesty especially well in consequence.'

Perhaps her most revealing comment about the family concerns her favourite of them all – the thirteenth-century adventurer Raoul Le Breton: 'A man after my own heart, an adventurous spirit who, in King John's reign, fought his way up the Seine with five hundred retainers to take Paris. I love Raoul for his pluck and enterprise and I cordially endorse his taste in desiring to possess so fascinating a city.

He pushed his way to the very gates of the citadel but, needless to say, his ambitious designs were there checked, and he and his bold followers captured. I am bound to add that Seigneur Raoul is insultingly referred to in French histories as 'The Channel Islands' Pirate'. I think it may have been this same Le Breton who gave a service of communion plate to the church of St. Brelade's where, I hope, it is still preserved. Possibly this gift was intended as an atonement for his piratical misdeeds.'

~

As for Lillie's parents, it was not their derring-do, but their looks which attracted admiration. Her English-born mother Emilie, after whom she herself was originally named, was petite, blue-eyed, auburn-haired, with a perfect complexion that she obviously handed down to her daughter. Charles Kingsley, author of *The Water Babies* and *Westward Ho* – described Emilie before her marriage as 'the most bewitchingly beautiful creature' he had ever seen. And, according to Lillie, the healthy outdoor life her mother led 'enabled her to retain much of her beauty to the end of her long life of eighty two years.'

Of Lillie's father, William Corbet, the Jersey Attorney-General H.E. Le V. dit Durrell wrote: 'His commanding presence, his genial personality, his suave manners, his gentle nature, his eloquent and poetic language tended to command admiration. He was the admired of all admirers, a gentleman in the best sense of the word. Even in Piccadilly people turned round to look at him.'

Lillie, too, remembered her father as 'a remarkably handsome man, and widely adored for his geniality and charm of disposition … His hair turned white at a very early age. Indeed, I never remember it otherwise. His eyes, very blue, looked through and through. He was over six feet in height, of rather ruddy complexion and majestic bearing, a characteristic which he retained throughout his life. I feel I cannot close this description of my Very Reverend father without a frivolous reference to his well-modelled limbs, which were vastly admired in the island and certainly did credit to his silk stockings he wore as Dean.'

Lillie with her parents and one of her brothers.

Recalling Lillie's own stage career, it is interesting that she adds, 'I am convinced that the Stage suffered a greater loss than the Army, for my father had the true histrionic gift, and his dramatic talent would have undoubtedly made him a fine actor. He had an extraordinarily retentive memory, which he trained so assiduously in learning by heart a certain amount of poetry each day that it became a difficult matter to find any English or Latin verse which he could not recite verbatim on the instant it was suggested.'

There is not, however, one mention thoughout Lillie's autobiography of the fact that the Dean had one fatal flaw – a weakness that she herself might have inherited and which, eventually, cost him his position as Dean of Jersey. The Very Reverend William Le Breton had an unbridled sexual appetite which led him into passionate relationships with women other than his wife.

2 Growing up in Jersey

VISITORS HAVE ALWAYS BEEN LAVISH in their praise of Jersey, with its fifty miles of varied coastline, its vividly coloured granite cliffs, its caves and coves, its twenty miles of sandy beaches and the charm of its tree-lined, narrow, winding lanes. When Lillie Le Breton was two-years-old, the exiled French writer, Victor Hugo, was expelled from Jersey, but he still found the Island 'ravissant'. The English novelist George Eliot, visiting Jersey two years later, wrote of: 'Such grassy vallies in this delicious island, with sleek cows turning mild faces on us as we pass them: such shadowy lanes and glimpses of the sea at unexpected openings.'

Lillie herself, when she was seventy and had travelled widely, fondly described the Jersey of her childhood: 'The climate is so mild that ixias, camellias, palms and geraniums flourish in the open air throughout the winter. The sky is intensely blue and the sea more violet than the Mediterranean. Indeed with its indented shores fashioned by nature into numberless small and beautiful bays with their stretches of golden sand, its country lanes with their high hedges topped by green aisles of arching trees, its apple orchards, its soft-eyed cattle browsing knee-deep in cool green valleys through which brooklets of clear water wander, and the comely milkmaids in native costume, the little Isle is certainly most attractive.'

It was in this rural environment, with a small market town to visit for shopping and special occasions, that Lillie Le Breton grew up and lived for the first twenty years of her life. Moreover, she was proud, too, of the elements which made her 'own little country' so unique. She lists them all: 'Its inhabitants are pure Norman, the Channel Islands being all that remain of the old Duchy of Normandy which conquered England ... We are not descendants of the English as the Canadians and Australians are, nor can we be considered as a British Colony, seeing that by ancient charter we are a self-governing political unit ... We have our own jurisdiction as well as our own assembly, or local parliament. This assembly, or States ... consists of the Lieutenant-Governor, Bailiff (the civil head), the Dean (ecclesiastical head) twelve jurats (aldermen) twelve rectors, twelve constables and fourteen deputies. It also includes the crown officers, who are allowed to speak, but not to vote.'

Lillie also pointed out that she, like most Islanders, was tri-lingual: not only did she speak French and English, but also Jersey Norman-French, a patois which so nearly resembles the Norman patois that, when travelling years later in Normandy, she noted, 'I found little difficulty in making myself intelligible.'

This pride in being politically independent and different in so many ways from both mainland England and France is a Jersey trait that Lillie certainly had in good measure and was a natural basis for the self-confidence that was later to be her hall-mark.

In *The Days I Knew* Lillie gives a vivid description of the happy childhood she and her six brothers enjoyed in Jersey. But, as she rarely dates any of her memories, it is difficult to discover what she did at any particular age. What is known, however, from other sources, is that, with beaches on the north, south, east and west coasts to choose from, she could swim when she was four and, with horses in the Deanery stables, ride by the time she was six.

As Lillie explains, their house was so large that 'One wing in the Deanery was set apart for the children, and there the younger of us romped, unhindered and to our heart's content, cared for by an old, white-haired nurse named Madame Bisson, vigorous and wholesome in the discharge of her duties and resplendent in a frilled cap, decorated with mauve ribbons.' This venerable

Jersey woman had a fund of good stories to keep the children enthralled. One was about the last French invasion of Jersey, when the French troops, cornered in the centre of St. Helier, were defeated in the Battle of Jersey in 1781. Madame Bisson's own father had actually witnessed the gallant Major Peirson routing the enemy from the Royal Square and even seen Lillie's great-grandmother flee with her children from this scene of bloody conflict in which both leaders were eventually killed.

But Madame Bisson's vivid recounting of how the French troops marched by night all the way from La Rocque on Jersey's south-east coast into the heart of St. Helier before they were discovered had, in Lillie's own words, 'a very disquieting effect upon childish minds and any unusual noises at night brought us bolt upright in bed, terrified at the possible return of our French enemies. There was no danger of such a happening but smuggling still continued, and Madame Bisson could give such a realistically accurate account of the smugglers' doings as eventually to create a suspicion that one of her sailor sons followed this particular calling.'

When Madame Bisson had her back turned and their parents were too busy to notice, there were all the pranks the Le Breton children got up to – Lillie included. 'Living the life of my brothers transformed me into an incorrigible tomboy. I could climb trees and vault fences with the best of them, and I entered with infinite relish into their practical jokes.' She wrote of her favourite escapades in detail and told of them with a sense of fun that comes to the surface again and again in her autobiography. There were their hauntings of St. Saviour's Churchyard: 'I have a lively recollection of my youngest brother and myself patrolling the old tree-shaded churchyard at midnight (when we were supposed to be in bed) mounted on stilts and draped in sheets, disquieting late passers-by very effectually. This prank continued until someone wrote to the Jersey papers, promising the ghosts at St. Saviour's graveyard a dose of cold lead if they appeared again.'

St. Saviour's Church

Then there was another game Lillie and Reggie enjoyed playing, which fortunately caused more amusement than anger: 'We two had always had an adoration for any quadruped that could be ridden or driven, from the moke up. When we were respectively eight and nine-years-old, we determined to make ourselves an equipment out of an old rumble, which was discovered in the corner of the coach house. The carpenter fitted it up somehow to please us, and to it we harnessed the lawn-mowing donkey, while, in order to lend dignity to the 'turn-out', a farm hand's little boy was engaged at a penny a week as groom, and sat with crossed arms in solemn state, nearly smothered in an old hat of my father's, with its distinguished ecclesiastical shape, and a discarded scarlet uniform coat belonging to one of my soldier brothers. It is a pity that there were no photographers at that moment to snap this unique conveyance, which caused so much mirth in the parish.'

Lillie and her brothers had, too, a passion for taking the door knockers off as many houses in St. Saviour's Parish as they could. 'We braved threats, dogs, enraged householders and even shotguns to obtain these trophies.' Once, though, this door knocker stealing was extended to playing with the door bell too.

The victim, old Mr. Wilkins, happened to live at the top of the lane leading to the Deanery and was always having tricks played on him by the inventive Le Breton children. This time, 'Having relieved him of his door knocker one evening, we tied a long, strong cord to his bell, making the other end fast to a stone, which we threw over a wall opposite with the result that everyone who passed, either on foot or on horseback, struck the cord, causing the old man's bell to ring furiously. At each fresh clanging, Wilkins emerged with the promptitude of a cuckoo clock striking the hour, and hurled the most violent language at the innocent wayfarers. Finally our audible chuckles behind the wall located the real culprits, and Wilkins preceded us to the deanery, where, after an interview with my father, fitting chastisement was inflicted upon us.'

Another practical joke they played was when some distinguished visitors were expected at the Deanery. There the guests all were, coming decorously up the drive, dressed in their best Albert coats and glossy top hats. What these guests did not see, though, was a cord stretched across the drive at hat level. As each guest approached the front door, the unseen cord knocked their hat off onto the dusty gravel path. Everyone seemed to suspect the cause was an overhanging branch from one of the trees lining the drive; no-one heard the suppressed giggles of the children hiding behind the trees. In later life Lillie would often tell this story, always concluding with the triumphant, 'You should have seen their faces!'

There was, too, the time when Lillie was impaled on the Deanery gate – all night. She and her brothers had been discovered in one of their night-time japes and ran swiftly back to the Deanery to get into their beds before their parents realised what they had been up to. Hampered by her skirt, Lillie reached home last and in her haste to climb the iron gate she usually scaled so easily, her foot slipped and part of her underclothing was caught on the spike at the top of the gate.

Lillie calmly reasoned that if she called out for help she would give the whole game away and get her brothers into trouble, so she just hung there on the gate all night, until she was rescued by a good friend of hers – the postman. Then she dashed round the back of the house and climbed into her bedroom through the window.

When Lillie told her brothers what had happened, they were astonished and it dawned on them how much their little sister had taken to heart what they had always tried to impress on her, the 'miserable handicap it was to be a girl, a silly creature, given to weeping on the slightest provocation, easily scared and full of qualms.' So this stoicism of Lillie's was ample proof that she had learnt the lesson that if she wanted to be allowed to take part in the boys' sports and not be left out in the cold. 'I must steady my nerves, control my tears, and look at things from a boy's point of view.'

She reacted with similar bravado when Reggie teased her that because she was a girl she would not dare to run naked down the often-used lane from the Deanery. Lillie immediately took on the dare, took off her clothes and ran as fast as she could down the lane and back into the Deanery – her long hair streaming behind her.

There was one escapade, however, that her mischievous brothers would not allow her to take part in: the tarring and feathering of the gilded statue of George II in the Royal Square in St. Helier. 'I shall never forget the tremendous and wrathful outburst which ensued when the townspeople discovered the outrage. It is an ill wind, however, which does not blow profit to some quarter, and an enterprising photographer coined money by snapping his spurious Majesty for souvenir purposes before scourers and painters had made him presentable again. Not infrequently, through our reputation for all manner of pranks, my brothers and I got the name without the fame, everything mischievous that was done being attributed off-hand to 'the dean's family'.'

Just as Lillie's unconventional upbringing allowed her more

Lillie as a young girl

physical freedom and outdoor activities than most other Jersey girls of her standing, so did her unusual tuition allow her to be better educated than most of the female contemporaries she was to meet with in later life. Naturally for those days, she was not sent to school as her brothers were – to nearby Victoria College. Her first teacher was a French governess, but Lillie confessed that, despite all the governess's attempts to teach her. 'I am afraid I was rather a handful.'

Lillie did much better with her brothers' tutor. He came to the Deanery every evening to supervise the boys' homework and it was he who taught her Latin, Greek and Mathematics. In addition she had lessons from German, French, music and drawing masters. No mention of needlework or household management! Lillie appreciated that she had had what amounted to a boy's education and acknowledged with gratitude 'My father was a remarkably clever and progressive man and believed firmly in the higher education of women.'

There was, though, a softer side to Lillie's nature too and this was shown when her pet canary died. All the Le Breton children had pets – rabbits, guinea pigs, ferrets – and they were each responsible for looking after their own. But Lillie completely forgot to feed her pet canary and it died of starvation. 'Filled with the deepest remorse, as I had every reason to be, I enclosed the unfortunate bird in a night-light box and buried it with funeral honours in a corner of the garden, inscribing on a wooden head-stone over the grave. 'Alas, poor Dick!' '

How did this tomboy at the Deanery appear to someone outside the family?

That same John Le Couteur who was alleged to have spoken disparagingly of Lillie's great-uncle the Bailiff, but who also happened to be ADC to Queen Victoria and the founder of the Royal Jersey Agricultural and Horticultural Society, mentioned her several times in his diary. When Lillie was ten he wrote of 'Mrs. Dean Le Breton and her pretty little girl'. After Lillie had a bad riding accident, he wrote disapprovingly of the freedom her parents allowed her: 'Called to hear how the Dean's daughter was. Imprudent to allow a girl of 13 to ride a racer with a snaffle.'

However, there is not so much of the tomboy in John Le Couteur's next two entries. In 1867 there is the entry: 'To call the Dean this morning at 11, to proceed to examine the lads at the Industrial School in St. Martins for my annual prize. Mrs. Le Breton and Lilly [sic], their pretty girl of 13 or 14, came with the Dean.' The second is: 'Took Mrs. Dean and pretty Lilly to their dressmaker.'

3   *The Lure of London*

SO IT SEEMS THAT ONCE Lillie was in her teens, she gradually turned to less tomboyish pursuits. She had always been a confirmed book worm, but at thirteen she also discovered the fascination of spiritualism and table-turning. In complicity with two other Jersey girls, Lillie became totally engrossed: 'One particular table which we used in our seances displayed such extraordinary agility, cut so many capers, and answered some of our questions so intelligently that I began to regard myself as a medium, and to feel that I really was, as the spirits we evoked assured me, the cause of these manifestations.' To the end of her life Lillie confessed that table-turning continued to attract and mystify her.

A year later there was the tale going round to suggest that she had inherited the profitable business sense that characterised most of her fellow Islanders: 'When I was about fourteen and my brother Reginald a year younger, we went halves in a weedy English mare that had run at the Gorey Annual Meeting without distinction. Flirt was put up to auction in the Jersey cattle market, where she was knocked down to Reggie's bid of thirty shillings! He brought her home, and stealthily installed her in a disused out-house, and we fed her as far as possible from the family stable bin. Her poor legs were in a sad condition, but with blistering and patience we got her fairly sound. I hacked her about the roads to divert suspicion, while my brother gave her real preparatory work, and we managed to land a selling plate of £30 with her the first time of asking – Reggie, of course, being "up".'

There were changes too in her family's circumstances which hastened Lillie's development from carefree girl to responsible young woman. For one thing, her five elder brothers, the instigators of the mad escapades, began to leave the Deanery for careers abroad; for another, her mother was not always well enough to carry out those tasks that normally fell to a Dean's wife. So Lillie began to accompany her father on his parochial duties and to Island functions – she even presented the prizes at school prize-givings. In Lillie's own words, 'I served as her substitute and did my share in visiting the sick and distressed.'

In the light of the world-wide acclaim her own beauty was to arouse, it is interesting to note that during this time Lillie remembered: 'I had occasionally stood and studied photographs of the recognised beauty, Lady Dudley, which had found their way into the little stationer's shop of St. Helier's in my quiet Island, and I sometimes wondered what it must be like to be such a great and fashionable beauty.'

Looking back to those teenage years, Lillie also admitted with typical frankness: 'I dare say thus being put forward a little prominently had the effect of making me rather precocious. At all events, when I approached my fourteenth year, I began to think that I should be included in invitations to the pleasant picnics and small informal dances which are a feature of Jersey social life. My mother agreed with me, and, in spite of my youth, I became her companion on these occasions. Going about as I did, it was impossible not to meet people older than myself and before I knew it, and to my bewilderment....I received my first proposal.'

Lillie's suitor was none other than Lieutenant Charles Spencer Longly, the twenty-three-year-old son of the Archbishop of Canterbury, stationed in Jersey with his regiment. He had been completely captivated by the young Lillie who not only had a fine complexion and pretty features, but who also looked the picture of robust health when on horseback. However, when Longly approached the Dean to ask for the hand of his daughter in marriage, he was astounded to be told that marriage was quite out of the question – Lillie was only fourteen-years-old. The dismayed Lieutenant immediately asked to be posted back to England.

There were one or two other suitors who approached Lillie, but she was no more impressed by them than she had been by Lieutenant Longly. She did admit, though, that such experiences 'had set my thoughts drifting into a new channel, and, like any other girl, I began to dream of the real Prince Charming who would one day appear.'

One place Prince Charming might appear – if he were not going to present himself in Jersey – was, of course, London. In fact, that mecca of English society, where a Queen and real Princes held court, had actually been suggested by Lord Suffield. He had a house in Jersey for a short period and, when he brought his family over to 'The Grove' in St. Lawrence, Lillie often went riding with his children. The suggestion came 'at one of those informal picnics in which Jerseyites delight' to which she had been invited. To begin with there was for Lillie an unexpected compliment, the first she ever remembered being paid to her: 'Do you know, Miss Le Breton, that you are very, very, beautiful?' Next followed the wonderful idea, 'You ought to have a season in London.'

The idea was not such an impossible one for Lillie to put into practice as it might have been for other Jersey girls, who often, in the whole of their lives, never left the Parish where they were born. Mrs. Le Breton still had relatives and connections in London and, because she was English, was quite used to the system of well-brought up young ladies completing their education with a season in town. The Dean, too, was known to several well-to-do families that were in London for the season.

Mrs. Le Breton and the sixteen-year-old Lillie, therefore, sailed from Jersey to Southampton and then travelled up to London with the promise of invitations to several places when they got there. The most prestigious was from Lord Suffield, for

them to dine with him at his home in Upper Grosvenor Street and then to attend the ball that followed.

Despite this genuine welcome to the capital, the visit was not, unfortunately, the social success that either Mrs. Le Breton or her daughter had dreamed of. Being the Dean of Jersey's daughter did not give Lillie the same prominence or attention that it did in Jersey. The St. Helier-made clothes that Lillie wore and her grown-up ways that so impressed her fellow Islanders made no impression whatsoever on the sophisticated Londoners whom they met.

The worst moment of all, as Lillie wrote later, was attending the Suffields' ball: 'When I walked into the ballroom, I felt like a clumsy peasant. My one 'party gown', which had been made for me in St. Helier, made me look like one of the serving maids. I had never waltzed, and could follow the leads of none of my dancing partners. The food was strange, and never having seen so many forks and spoons at one's supper place, I had no idea which to use. I disgraced myself so often I could scarcely wait until the evening came to its abysmal end.' Both mother and daughter were forced to admit that Lillie was not ready for London, nor London for her – yet.

For Lillie their return to Jersey meant a return to Deanery duties and the usual Island round of bazaars, fêtes, picnics, enlivened by rides with Reggie along the beaches and through the country lanes but, also, as Lillie wrote later, by evenings when she would read Shakespeare's plays out aloud with her father: 'Between the ages of sixteen and twenty I learned the magic of words, the beauty and excitement of poetic imagery. I learned there was something in life other than horses, the sea, and the long Jersey tides.' So that is how Lillie spent the next four years, until 1873, when her brother William married Miss Elizabeth Anne Price, daughter of Mr. Francis Price of Trinity. And what a grand affair the wedding turned out to be, as well as an unexpected turning point in Lillie's life.

The Dean himself married the pair in his own Church of St.

Saviour; Lillie was one of the four bridesmaids, while her youngest brother Reggie was one of the four groomsmen. The *British Press* and *Jersey Times* painted the picture of that November wedding in glowing terms:

> St Saviour's Church and Hill have not been so gay for many a day as they were last evening when thousands flocked to the Church to see a fashionable marriage. This ceremony had been much talked of for some days previously, and being at evening instead of the orthodox morning, and their being rumours of a torch light procession and other wonderful things the crowd was greater than is usual on such occasions. The ceremony was fixed, for six o'clock, and true to the hour it commenced.

Lillie and the other bridesmaids wore ruby red satin tunics over white grenadine dresses – made by Mrs. Boielle of Bath Street and Miss Curtis of Colomberie – and Louis Quinze hats of ruby red silk, trimmed with pearls and long white ostrich feathers. As the reporter enthused: 'The effect of the rich ruby colours, the pearls and long ostrich feathers by gas light may be easily imagined; it was a truly pretty sight.'

The reporter next tried to capture some of the excitement caused by this important event in Jersey's social calendar: 'A host of friends of both bride and bridegroom were present , and the outside public, attracted by the sight, was multitudinous. Indeed so great was the crowd that the church, the churchyard near the path leading from the gate to the porch of the church, the road, the adjacent walls were crowded. The crush was terrific. Individually walking was impossible; collectively the crowd clung to the pillars, stepped upon each other; outside, the disorder was greater, rendered none the less so by the numberless carriages in waiting. When the ceremony was over a passage from the porch of the church to the gate was kept by the yachtsmen of the *Red Gauntlet* who carried the so-called 'torches' – carriage lamps – which they had waved over their heads thus affording light to

Edward Langtry

the wedding party. Lamps were also suspended to the adjacent trees. Those lamps shining upon the brilliant colours in the attire of the bride and bridemaids made the effect exceedingly beautiful'.

The whole splendid ceremony was concluded with a dinner given by the bride's father in his Trinity home. To the dinner, Lillie as bridesmaid was, of course, invited. So also was the bride's brother-in-law, Edward Langtry, whose wife, the bride's sister, had died tragically of tuberculosis after two years of marriage. Here was a dinner-party, not in distant London but in familiar Jersey, at which Lillie could naturally shine and the light of her beauty shone directly on the widower, Edward Langtry.

After this dinner in Trinity, there was still more merry-making to come. As William's best man, Edward Langtry gave a ball in honour of the bride and groom at the Jersey Yacht Club: 'It was a far more elaborate and extravagant affair than anything I had hitherto witnessed, and it electrified me. The walls were hung with quantities of flags; the supper was less sketchy than I had been accustomed to, and, to crown all, the hall and staircase were lined with sailors in their spotless white suits. To me, it was simply dazzling, an Arabian Night's entertainment, and its donor instantly became in my eyes a wonder!' Edward's final gesture was to loan the happy couple the use of his luxurious eighty-foot yacht the *Red Gauntlet* for their honeymoon. No wonder Lillie was so impressed by what must have seemed evidence of untold wealth.

More was to follow – for when the *Red Gauntlet* was returned, Edward took Lillie, with the Dean as chaperon, on sailing trips round the Island, even taking her on one occasion to France for the day. Edward was obviously as much impressed by Lillie as she was by his generosity. The Dean, however, did not look so favourably on Edward as a suitor as Lillie did; her mother was loath to lose her only daughter – at least before she had had a successful London season; Reggie, her only brother still at home, regarded the lack-lustre Edward as a most unsuitable match for his spirited sister and refused to take any part in encouraging the relationship.

But, as Lillie remembered, 'the stronger the opposition, the more determined I grew.' So within six weeks of their meeting, Lillie was able to accept Edward's proposal of marriage – 'I thought myself desperately in love' – and proudly wore his expensive diamond engagement ring. With it she scratched her maiden name, as some kind of remembrance, on the window of her old schoolroom in the Deanery.

The wedding itself was arranged for March. With her usual determination, Lillie – with the time of high tide a useful ally – saw to it that her wedding in no way followed the pattern of William's grand marriage festivities. 'I hated the idea of a big wedding and the conventional bridal array.' Her father and her brother Clement saw to the business side of the marriage. Lillie was to have a settlement from Edward's father – a wealthy Belfast shipowner – of £10,000; she would have the interest to live off during Edward's life-time and the capital sum on his death.

Early on the morning of 9th March 1874, the twenty-year-old Lillie Le Breton – plainly dressed in her going away outfit – married the twenty-six-year-old Irishman Edward Langtry (of independent means) in St. Saviour's Church by special licence. The Dean of Jersey took the ceremony, but the only one of her brothers present was Clement. Trevor and Francis had died abroad; Maurice and William were both in India – Reggie preferred to go riding that day. After a quiet wedding breakfast at the Yacht Club, the newly married pair caught the high-tide and sailed away on the *Red Gauntlet*. Could Lillie have been serious when, many years later, she claimed: 'To become the mistress of the yacht, I married the owner.'?

The newly-weds spent most of the summer sailing, first on the *Red Gauntlet* – until Edward had to sell her to raise money – and then on the eighty-ton racing yawl the *Gertrude*. Their relationship was perhaps at its best during these first months: 'I entered with him into the sport of yachting', Lillie remembered, especially when the *Gertrude* won, among other races, the International Yacht Race at Le Havre: 'How I enjoyed the excitement of that race, crowding on sail to the verge of danger, with a swirling spray drenching us to the skin.'

But it was from mixing with the yachting fraternity that Lillie also learned an important lesson. She gained an appreciation of the power exerted by the owners of large yachts, no matter what their origins. She also determined that, one day, 'I would become one of them.'

When not on board, the Langtrys' had two pied a terres. The first was in Jersey. No doubt seeking to re-enact the way of life enjoyed by her Le Breton forbears when they had been Seigneurs of Jersey, Lillie persuaded Edward to choose Noirmont Manor, where the family had formerly had their feudal seat. The Manor itself had been rebuilt in 1810 and had to recommend it a specially fine staircase leading from the elegant reception rooms; an ancient camellia bush in the grounds – one of the first to be planted in Jersey; and, above all, breath-taking views across St. Aubin's Bay to St. Helier. Lillie's additions to the house while they were there were a bath and, of course, her signature – 'Lillie Langtry' this time – on one of the window panes.

It is from Noirmont that Lillie also started writing to Arthur Jones, the illegitimate son of Lord Ranelagh, who lived in Portelet House, St. Brelade. In this, the first of sixty-six recently discovered letters that Lillie fondly wrote to him throughout his life, she merely thanked this fellow parishioner for his present of a cake.

In England there was the Elizabethan mansion that Edward had bought, overlooking Southampton Water. It was staffed by four servants, including a butler to whom Lillie willingly handed over the day to day running of the house. When Lillie eventually tired of the too familiar social round in Jersey, the Langtrys moved permanently to Edward's Cliffe Lodge. Here it was that she caught the nineteenth century scourge – the acute, highly infectious disease that affected all classes of people, from the Prince of Wales himself to the paupers begging in the streets – typhoid.

Lillie lay seriously ill for nearly a month and her worried doctor prescribed a change of scene to stimulate her recovery. As she herself said: 'I have no idea what led us to select the great smoky city as a sanatorium', but, nonetheless, the Langtrys chose, for the sake of Lillie's health, to leave Southampton for London. To her mother Lillie wrote, 'We leave for London early in December, and, after stopping at an hotel for a day or two, we shall take suitable apartments.'

So, by January 1876, Cliffe Lodge had been put up for sale and the Langtrys had rented accommodation in Eaton Place, Belgravia. They spent the rest of the year uneventfully: Lillie passing the long hours with nothing better to do than reading in bed; Edward feeling, as Lillie put it, 'quite like a fish out of water', made up for the loss of his much preferred outdoor pursuits by drinking. Both were completely ignored by the society crowd that Lillie so envied. It was not until the following year that London gave Lillie what she had really been looking for – recognition.

4 The Finger of Fate

IT WAS A TELEGRAM FROM Jersey on 17th December, 1876, that first broke into this lethargy of the Langtrys. Reggie, Lillie's youngest brother and her close companion throughout her childhood, had died suddenly from congestion of the lungs. Lillie immediately started to travel back to St. Helier for the funeral: 'the interminable journey to Jersey during which I lay weeping all night.' For, after Lillie's engagement to Edward nearly three years earlier, her favourite brother had been more than distant: he had refused to be present at her wedding, to visit her at Noirmont Manor, to answer her letters from London. They had not met since the morning of her wedding day.

To add to her guilt and grief, Lillie arrived too late to attend Reggie's funeral: 'All these things made me feel that life was over. I returned to London in a state of deep depression, caring little for anything.' This was in the spring of 1877 and, as Lillie remembered: 'We passed time as country cousins do – walking in the Park watching for royalty to pass, for I had never set eyes on even a minor one, and in going to museums and picture galleries, seeing many interesting things that were new to me and which, although I still felt very sad, made me feel a little more contented with life.' In fact, one day the Langtrys did see the Prince of Wales, on horseback, as Lillie described in a letter to her mother: 'He is a very large man, but appeared to ride well for one of his bulk.'

Yet, as Lillie confessed years later, she was still possessed by the conviction that her destiny lay in London: 'I can offer no logical explanation for my feeling, but know only that not even the uneventful tenor of my life could rid me of it.' Then, quite unexpectedly, the moment came. Lillie's fortunes did change, and all because of a chance meeting with someone she had first known in Jersey. 'It must have been the finger of Fate,' she later claimed, 'that one afternoon a fortnight after my return, pointed the way to the Aquarium at Westminster. It had been newly opened, and was a popular resort at the moment, and there in the crowd we came across Lord Ranelagh.'

The result of this surprise meeting between two people, who had as their common bond former residence in Jersey, was twofold. Straightaway the Ranelaghs asked the Langtrys to stay with them for a few days at their house in Fulham. Then, at the prompting of Lord Ranelagh, came their first invitation to an important social occasion in London: 'A card arrived for a Sunday evening at-home from Lady Sebright, a very enthusiastic amateur actress, fond of literature and art, and who loved to gather at these Sunday eve-ning receptions men and women conspicuous in both callings, besides a purely social element.'

Everything that Lillie might have thought would count against her when she was set among a crowd of such brilliant people did, in fact, only enhance her presence – but not at the start of the evening. 'We rattled up to Lady Sebright's house in Lowndes Square in a humble four-wheeler. Being, of course, in deep mourning, I wore a very simple black, square-cut gown (designed by my Jersey modiste) with no jewels – I had none – or ornaments of any kind, and with my hair twisted carelessly on the nape of my neck in a knot.' So it was with some trepidation that Lillie and Edward slipped into the Sebrights' drawing-room and were presented to the hostess. Introductions over, Lillie 'retired shyly to a chair in a remote corner, feeling very unsmart and countrified.'

For the second time in a month, Lillie was to owe a sudden change in her circumstances to the encouraging experience of meeting someone who knew Jersey. This time it was John Millais, the most eminent English painter of his day. Millais had actually been born in Southampton, but he had spent most of his boyhood – nearly fifty years before – in St. Helier. So when he realised where this young, unusually dressed and beautiful woman had come from, he 'beamed in friendly enthusiasm while he claimed me as his countrywoman.'

But Millais was not the only person to be led to the Langtrys remote corner of the drawing room by the energetic Lady Sebright. 'Among other notabilities whom I met on that (to me) memorable occasion, who afterwards became my firm friends, were James McNeill Whistler, the famous American artist (who had wonderful, speaking hands); Henry Irving (approaching the zenith of his fame); Lord Wharncliffe, made rich by finding coal on his Sheffield property and wisely spending the surplus on art collection and art encouragement; Abraham Hayward, the well-known essayist; Frank Miles, the artist; and William Yardley, an amateur actor and leading cricketer of the day.'

Despite several other requests for the honour, it was Millais who eventually took Lillie down to supper. 'I was glad, for I was fearfully shy, and his gay assumption of kinsmanship made me feel more at ease with him than with others I had met that evening.' While they were at supper, as well as delighting to speak to Lillie in Jersey Norman-French, Millais asked her a completely unexpected question. Would she sit for him? He – one of the famed Pre-Raphaelite Brotherhood – wanted to be the first painter to reproduce on canvas what he called the 'classic features' of his countrywoman. By the end of the evening, the young artist Frank Miles had gone further – he had already made some lightning sketches of this captivating newcomer to Lady Sebright's circle.

After this first and overwhelming introduction to London society, life for the Langtrys – who had now been married for three years – was never to be the same again. The very next day their landlady at Eaton Place was complaining about the number of people coming to her door with invitations for them; soon Frank Miles' sketches of Lillie were put on sale in London shops, spreading the fame of her unusual beauty; before long Millais' engraving of Lillie as Effie Deans, the ill-fated heroine in Scott's *The Heart of Midlothian*, was to attract attention; Sir Edward Poynter asked her to sit for him; George Watts wanted to paint her as 'The Dean's Daughter'; photographers begged to be allowed to take her portrait to be displayed in their shop windows.

Yet, Lillie made no attempt to copy either the ornate dresses, or the elaborate hairstyles, of the other so called Professional Beauties, P.B.s for short. For every social engagement she put on the same plain, black dress – made by Madame Nicolle of St. Helier as suitable mourning attire after the death of her brother Reggie. She still wore her hair brushed loose, or simply twisted into a knot at the back of her head – soon to be known and copied as the 'Langtry' knot. So what exactly was her special attraction?

Her special attraction was that she was different and dared to remain so. She came from an Island about which most people had never heard; as an Anglican Dean's daughter she was acceptable to aristocratic circles – after all, her brother Clement was later to marry Lord Ranelagh's daughter – but her upbringing and education had in no way been similar to that of her mainland contemporaries; though her regular features appealed to the artists of the day, she had nothing in common with the pallid, languorous models usually favoured by the Pre-Raphaelites. Most importantly, she still retained the sense of fun, the love of an active life, that had been encouraged by her brothers, plus an independent spirit that no doubt came from her being a Jersey woman.

The admirers of her unique qualities were not just painters though: they included peers of the realm, prime ministers, poets, playwrights, even the President of the United States, Theodore Roosevelt, who said 'She's so pretty she takes away a man's breath.' So the tributes to Lillie were both legion and perceptive.

She had 'dewy violet eyes, a complexion like a peach; quite simply the most beautiful woman on earth'; the full-breasted, broad-hipped Lillie walked 'like a beautiful hound set upon its feet.'

The Countess of Warwick questioned, 'How can words convey the vitality, the glow, the amazing charm that made this fascinating woman the centre of any group she entered?' Oscar Wilde, too, exclaimed about 'her calm, her wit and her mind – what a mind!' No less a radical thinker than George Bernard Shaw complained 'she has no right to be intelligent, daring and independent as well as lovely.' Edward Michael also noted that Lillie possessed 'far more heart than she was given credit for.'

The painting which best captures the character and attraction of the twenty-four-year-old Lillie at this time – also her own favourite – was Millais' portrait of her as he first met her. He insisted on her wearing her simple black dress, her hair knotted back, with – for a touch of colour – a crimson Jersey lily in her hand. The lily sent from St. Helier to serve as a model was actually, by mistake, the Guernsey lily, but the finished portrait was still entitled 'A Jersey Lily'.

While Lillie was sitting for Millais in his new studio in Palace Gate, he told her she was the most exasperating subject he had ever painted. 'I looked just beautiful for about fifty-five out of every sixty minutes, but for five in every hour I was amazing.' When the portrait was finally hung in the Royal Academy in 1878, it drew such throngs of people that it had to be roped off to prevent it being damaged. In 1879, 1890 and again in 1920 – when Lillie was nearly seventy – the portrait was nominated the picture of the year. The portrait's title, 'A Jersey Lily', soon became one that Lillie was only too proud and happy to accept for herself.

Lillie's comments on that astounding first London season – when there was scarcely a great house she did not visit – are revealing both about her own response to it and also about her fading rapport with her unfortunate husband, who was unwillingly dragged from one function to another, merely as an acceptable token of propriety. 'Whatever my husband said and felt, I absolutely revelled in the novelty of it all.' It also taught her another lesson which was later to stand her in good stead.

'While I carried away with me from these functions a general sense of pomp and grandeur, there was a simplicity about the people which one finds only in those born to greatness, or who have achieved it.'

News of Lillie's London success eventually reached Jersey, where there were three young girls at Government House most eager to catch a glimpse of the famous Mrs. Langtry. They were Ada Norcott, the Lieutenant-Governor's daughter and the two Sutherland sisters, the youngest of whom was to grow up into another celebrated Jersey beauty – the red-haired temptress Elinor Glyn. Lillie was back in Jersey visiting her father the Dean and had been invited to dine with the Norcotts. In her autobiography *The Romantic Adventure*, Elinor tells what happened next:

Ada and Lucy and I hid under the dressing-table in the room where she would have to leave her cloak, so as to get a glimpse of her. The table was covered with pink glazed calico, and hung with muslin, and greatly daring we cut three little peep-holes in the calico. One of us giggled with excitement at her arrival, and we were soon discovered, but she was kind and sweet, and merely laughed and pulled us out, promising not to give us away. Perhaps she felt flattered by so touching a proof of earnest admiration even from three unimportant little girls. I can see her now as she went down the stairs, her wonderfully blue eyes smiling as she kissed her hand to us. She wore a white corded silk dress, with a tight bodice and a puffed-up bustle at the back. The low neck was square-cut, with a stitched pleating round the edge, and her elbow-sleeves had lace frills. Her golden-brown hair was worn in a curled fringe in front like the Du Maurier drawings, and was tied at the back with a bright scarlet ribbon bow en catogan. She was the first grown-up person we had ever seen who did not wear a chignon … Her kindness extended to a plea that we might be allowed to share some of the party dishes.

'A Jersey Lily' by Millais

But there was, too, an unpleasant side to becoming a celebrity overnight. Everyone was only too eager to catch a glimpse of the lovely Mrs. Langtry: at Lady Jersey's reception many of the guests stood up on chairs; strollers in Hyde Park would go so far as to lift her sunshade; shoppers blocked doorways when they learned she was inside; crowds surged round to watch her mount for her daily ride in Rotten Row. As Lillie herself put it: 'To better illustrate my predicament I may state as a fact that, one Saturday afternoon, a young girl, with an aureole of fair hair and wearing a black gown, was seated in the park near the Achilles statue.

Someone raised the cry that it was I, people rushed towards her and, before the police could interfere, she was mobbed to such an extent that an ambulance finally conveyed her, suffocating and unconscious to St. George's Hospital.'

So there were many simple amusements she had enjoyed while a nobody, that she had now to do without. Moreover, Edward 'greatly disliked all this publicity, sometimes losing his temper and blaming me! As can be readily understood, his position was an onerous one, for, aside from the vexation of seeing his wife stared at as a species of phenomenon, we never went out but that he was kept busy hurrying me from one place to another as he saw the familiar crowds beginning to assemble.'

Nevertheless, Lillie still considered all that was happening to her as 'a marvel'. Even when – out of deference to Lord Dudley's aversion to black – she entered the Dudley House ballroom wearing a classically severe white velvet dress and caused such a sensation that the other guests stopped dancing to look at her, she still felt like a 'country girl'; someone who 'had not been allowed by my band of brothers to think much of myself in any way.'

There was, however, one social accolade that had not yet been bestowed on Lillie – she had never been introduced to the Prince of Wales. Bertie, as he was affectionately known to his friends, though heir to the throne and already thirty-five, was allowed by his mother, Queen Victoria, to play no useful part in the matters of Monarchy. So he spent most of his time with his 'Marlborough Set', living the carefree life of a wealthy landowner. Although the beautiful Danish princess Alexandra had been chosen as a suitable wife for him and had given him five children, he continued in his bachelor ways and she had had to resign herself to accepting his extrovert life style and his weakness for attractive women.

The eventual meeting of the heir to the throne and the most arresting woman of her day was arranged by Sir Allen Young, a wealthy bachelor who had devoted part of his life to searching for the North-West Passage. Lillie could only remember feeling 'panic-stricken' as the Prince was brought towards her to be introduced, while she and her husband stood by the drawing-room fireplace, the only newcomers at this party given by Sir Allen.

For one bewildering minute, apparently, Lillie even 'considered the advisability of climbing the chimney to escape, but, my presence of mind returning, I stood my ground and made my curtsey, after which, again for various reasons, I greatly enjoyed watching my husband go rather stammeringly through a similar ordeal.' She was equally nervous when it came to the supper. She was put next to the Prince of Wales 'who, however, extracted only monosyllabic replies either from myself or my husband, the latter being even more dumb than I was.' But silent though she may have been, Lillie was 'immensely interested in watching the Prince, and soon realised that, while good-natured and pleasant to everyone, he preserved his dignity admirably ... He displayed a sincere fondness for Sir Allen Young, praised his cook, and seemed bent on making the evening a jolly one; but this remarkable consideration for his host and hostess, I discovered subsequently, was always apparent. He really worked to make one's dinners and parties successful – an easy task with his magnetic personality.'

Lillie's obvious approval of His Royal Highness was entirely reciprocated. Soon after the small supper party at Stratford Place, Lillie was seen riding her fine thoroughbred 'Redskin' – a present from the wealthy young landowner Moreton Frewer – strikingly dressed in a tight-fitting black habit. Her companion in Hyde Park was the Prince of Wales.

5 The Seal of Royal Approval

LILLIE HAD ALREADY BEEN INTRODUCED to Queen Victoria's youngest son, Prince Leopold. She found him 'a tall transparent-skinned young man, of gentle manners and extreme simplicity, artistic and of marked intellectuality', though, sadly, 'rather delicate and often ill.' She met the young Prince at parties given by his intimate friends; he was also a frequent visitor to Eaton Place; he had even hung one of Miles' pencil drawings of her over his bed at Buckingham Palace, only to have it snatched down by his disapproving mother. But their simple friendship obviously never made the stir that Lillie's public appearance in the company of his eldest brother, the Prince of Wales, now did.

It would seem that the heir to the throne had inherited from the more lusty of his royal forbears the same voracious sexual appetite that was so soon to ruin the reputation of William Le Breton, the Dean of Jersey. For the fifteen years of Bertie's marriage to the beautiful but increasingly deaf and supposedly frigid Alexandra, he had been unfaithful with every pretty woman he fancied. Prostitute or aristocrat – it was all the same to him, but he dallied with no one for long. In 1870 – while Lillie was still in Jersey – Bertie had even had to appear as a witness in a divorce suit filed by Sir Charles Mordaunt against his wife. The Prince of Wales, though it was known that he had written Lady Harriet letters and called on her in private, stoutly denied 'any improper familiarity or criminal act' between them.

Now, however, for the first time in his life, he only had eyes for one woman – the lively Lillie Langtry. She became his 'Fair

Lily', his Royal Mistress. So from that May in 1877, the Langtrys' social diary closely followed Bertie's unvarying annual routine: the summer centred round the royal couple's London home, Marlborough House; Cowes in August for the sailing; Scotland in October for the grouse shooting and deer stalking; most of the winter months in Sandringham for more shooting; with March devoted to the Prince's beloved France, when he divided his time between Paris and the Riviera.

How did the Princess of Wales and Edward Langtry react to this open and public relationship between their spouses? Queen Victoria had already summed up her Danish daughter-in-law as 'good, so simple, unaffected, frank, bright and cheerful, yet so quiet and gentle' – but, 'very clever I don't think she is.' The Queen had to admit, too, 'She is very fond of Bertie, but not blind.'

Princess Alexandra, in fact, made no fuss and simply called her errant husband 'my naughty little man.' To Lillie herself she showed nothing but genuine kindness. Lillie often told the tale of the Princess' reaction when she was suddenly taken ill at a Marlborough House dinner party: 'The Princess, so considerate and compassionate always, immediately told me to hurry home to bed, which I thankfully did. Half an hour later the Household Physician, Francis Laking, was ushered into my room, having been sent by command of the Princess of Wales to see me and report to her on my condition. By the next afternoon I was feeling better, and was lying on the sofa in my little drawing room about tea-time, when the butler suddenly announced Her Royal Highness, who entered, followed by her inseparable secretary, Miss Charlotte Knollys.

The honour of the unexpected visit brought me at once to my feet, ill though I felt, but the Princess insisted on my lying down again, while she made herself tea, chatting kindly and graciously. She always used a specially manufactured violent scent, and I recall exclaiming on the delicious perfume, and her solicitous answer that she feared possibly that it was too strong for me.'

Edward Langtry, who – at Lillie's insistence and perhaps on

the advice of Bertie's multi-millionaire friend Freake – had agreed to their moving from Eaton Place to a more elegant house in Norfolk Street, just off Park Lane, had little choice in the matter. As Lillie's lawful husband he was still expected in public to accompany his wife to all the social functions he so hated and in private to accept with dignity, and perhaps some pride, her liaison with the heir to the throne. When this dual role became too onerous, he went away on fishing trips, visited America, or stayed at home taking solace in drinking. But both the mores of the period and Edward's own temperament would have made it unthinkable for him to have sought to divorce Lillie on the grounds of her adultery.

This meant that Lillie and Bertie were free to live lives purely for their own pleasure and to enjoy matching their own boundless vitality with that of their chosen companion. Lillie appreciated the Prince's warm-heartedness, his genuine desire to please and the delight he took in being surrounded by happy, smiling faces. The Prince appreciated Lillie's brightness as much as her beauty; her love of practical jokes as well as of fine clothes; her ability to adorn sophisticated society one minute and vigorously join in outdoor pursuits the next. But, above all, the Prince valued Lillie's sturdy independence, her refusal to be subservient, which enabled this delightfully different young woman from Jersey to avoid being a sycophantic hanger-on and to become a true friend.

So Lillie and Bertie spent their time together in 1877 and 1878 in several different places, taking part in many varied activities. There were dawn rides in Hyde Park, even if Lillie had just got home from a ball; there were also the fashionable evening rides when Margot Asquith remembered how 'in a shining top-hat and skin-tight habit, she rode a chestnut thoroughbred of conspicuous action every evening in Rotten Row.' The Prince (with other members of his circle) was frequently her riding companion. At Cowes – with Bertie and his family living on his yacht *Osborne* and the Langtrys the guests of Sir Allen Young on his schooner *Helen* – there were daily sailing

Dressed for the theatre.

competitions, as well as 'the cruising in floating palaces by day and the dances on shore at night … a whirlwind of gaiety.'

1877 happened to be the first year that the Prince of Wales raced horses under his own colours of purple with scarlet sleeves, so that summer he enthusiastically took Lillie the round of Newmarket, Ascot and Goodwood. With matching enthusiasm, no doubt fuelled by memories of the outdoor life in Jersey she had so enjoyed, Lillie revelled in this whole new experience: 'As far as I'm concerned the pleasures of the turf do not merely consist in owning horses and seeing them win. I like the routine of racing. The fresh air, the picnic lunch, the rural surroundings, all tend to make a race meeting a delightful outing.' In July especially, 'After the rush and fatigue of a London season, it was a heavenly relief to find oneself under the beautiful trees of Goodwood Park.'

In Leicestershire, as the guest of Lord Manners, Lillie tried riding to hounds but, in the end, found it easier to follow the hunt on a docile hack rather than astride a high-spirited hunter. She attended a winter ball at Sandringham, staying for the sake of propriety with the Romneys, rather than at Sandringham House itself. Her comment on the experience? 'While a very spacious house, Sandringham is not palatial, but what is far better, it gives one the idea of being thoroughly livable and comfortable, even when turned partially upside-down for a dance.'

Her first visit to Scotland she described 'a revelation'. The Langtrys were part of Cunliffe Brooks' large house party at Glen Tanar in the Highlands. The men, Lillie noted, 'eager for the massacre of grouse and the stalking of deer...enjoyed themselves hugely killing things, but there is nothing much for women to do unless they also shoulder a weapon.' She confessed, however, that this had never appealed to her 'I have always felt it to be a woman's mission to give life, rather than take it. I was once persuaded to see a stag stalked, but I felt so sick and sorry for the fine beast that I have never forgotten it.' Thankfully, though, Lillie did find that 'there is no place like Scotland to bring roses to a woman's cheeks', and took an eager part in all the Highland reels and scottisches that made the evenings so much more enjoyable than the days.

Then there was all the fun: Lillie's imitation of a crowing cock in the middle of a dinner party; her sliding down the stairs at Glen Tanar on a silver tray; her taking part in a spot of spirit rapping in Mrs. Oust's cottage at Cowes, when the 'moving spirit' turned out to be none other than the French Prince Imperial 'hard at work throwing the furniture about!' Bertie's preferences were for apple pie beds; stuffing friends' pockets with sticky sweets, or squirting them with water from a bicycle pump; having pies filled with mustard instead of custard. It was obvious to any onlooker that the two of them unconsciously shared the same uninhibited *joie de vivre*.

It did not take Bertie long after his first meeting with Lillie to decide to have a house specially built for her. He wanted somewhere well away from London where they could spend time quietly together just like any ordinary middle-class couple. They chose Bournemouth and they called their mock Tudor house – a style much favoured by the Victorians – 'The Red House', because of its red brick base. Its foundation stone bore, beside the date 1877, the carved initials E.L.L., – combining both Lillie's maiden and married names – Emilie Le Breton Langtry. In the Bournemouth register of leaseholders, however, Lillie's name was given as Emily Charlotte Langton, to protect her anonymity.

Inside the house, E.L.L. appeared again, this time as part of the carved oak mantelpiece in the dining room. In the same room, two amorous swans were depicted in the stained glass window, while high upon one of the walls were the dismissive words 'They say – what say they? Let them say.' The house also had its own motto, painted along a wooden beam in the entrance hall: 'And yours, too, my friend.'

Upstairs, on the opposite side of the house to her own, was the Prince's suite of rooms. They were the most imposing in the whole house, as the reception rooms were furnished unostentatiously for private comfort rather than for public show.

Above: 'The Red House', Bournemouth, now the Langtry Manor Hotel.
Below: King Edward VII own Suite. Note Millais' portrait of Lillie hanging on the chimney breast.

On an outside wall of this suite was the Latin tag *Stet Fortuna Demesis* – 'May Fortune attend those who dwell here' . On the outside wall of Lillie's suite was the modest *Dulce Domum* – 'Sweet Home'. There was also a balcony leading from her suite, where the pair could relax over afternoon tea and enjoy the view across to the English Channel.

Even this royal gift did not escape Lillie's sense of fun. On an upstairs window were two mock coats of arms: under one were the words 'Ye Armes of Ye Britaines', under the other 'Ye Armes of Ye Romanes'. Here, in the Red House, was a refuge for Bertie from the pomposity of court life and for them both a respite from the boredom of loveless marriages. For the two of them it was like 'playing at houses' .

As a token of his appreciation of all that Lillie meant to him, Bertie arranged that, during her second London season, Lillie would be granted her wish – to be presented to the Queen. The first correct step for him to take was to present Edward Langtry to Queen Victoria at one of her levees in March. That done, the Prince saw to it that Lillie's sponsor for her own presentation two months later was a favoured member of the Queen's household, Lady Conyngham. Her companion for the actual day was to be Lady Romney.

Bertie's final gesture was to send Lillie a bouquet of Maréchal Neil roses, whose pale yellow petals exactly matched the lining of the long court train of her ivory brocade gown. Lillie's own final touch was to wear in her hair three of the longest ostrich feathers she could find.

She had heard that the Queen had recently complained of the 'tiny' feathers – meant to represent the royal *fleur de lys* – that women were wearing when they were presented to her and she was determined not to make the same mistake.

Both her mother and her aunt were in London to help Lillie dress for this special occasion, but they had a sudden disagreement as to whether Lillie should eat beforehand or not. 'My aunt thought I ought to have lunch before I started, or I should surely faint, but my mother affirmed that if I ate anything I should certainly have a red nose, and as my aunt had never been to Court and my mother had, the latter gained the day and I starved accordingly.'

But, as they saw it, that was not the end of her mother's and aunt's duties. 'They rehearsed me in the catching of my train as it would be thrown to me by the pages after my presentation and also made me practise the royal curtsey until my knees ached. They warned me on no account to glance over my shoulder to see if my train was being properly spread by the pages in attendance, for that would be a sign that I was a country cousin, and so on and so on.'

At last the moment came when Lillie was to hand her train to the pages, 'in my grandest manner' and, as the Lord Chamberlain announced 'Mrs. Langtry comes next, your Majesty', approach the royal presence. Then, without committing any of the indiscretions against which her mother had warned her, Lillie curtsied and kissed Queen Victoria's hand:

'It seemed to me an amazing thing to be shown into the presence of a sovereign one had heard of and prayed for all one's life and to approach near enough to bend forward and kiss her hand, and though the experience lasted but a second , I thrilled with emotion, loyalty, and pride. The Queen's wonderful dignity made me unable to realise that she was a petite woman, and she appeared to me to be the very embodiment of majesty.

She was dressed quite simply, in black, of course, with low neck and short sleeves, and her train was of velvet. Across her bodice was the blue ribbon of the Garter, and diamond orders and jewels studded her corsage. She wore many strings of beautiful pearls round her neck, a small diamond crown, tulle veil, and black feathers forming her head-dress.'

As the Queen's hand was being kissed by the woman whose picture she had taken down from over her youngest son's bed, by the adulteress who was the publicly acknowledged mistress of her eldest son, Lillie could not help noticing that Queen Victoria looked straight in front of her and extended her hand in a rather perfunctory manner: 'There was not even the flicker of a smile on her face, and she looked grave and tired.' That, however, as far as Lillie was concerned, was not really important. What did matter was that at last she had been given that ultimate seal of royal approval – she had been presented at Court. Now she could be invited anywhere by anyone from the top echelons of the social hierarchy and that included being asked to attend the receptions and balls held at Buckingham Palace itself. For her, 'the balls at Buckingham Palace completely realised my girlish dreams of fairyland.'

Lillie remembered in later life these halcyon days as 'a dream, a delight, a wild excitement.' She admitted with endearing frankness, too, 'I concentrated on the pursuit of amusement with the whole-heartedness that is characteristic of me, flying from one diversion to another from dawn to dawn, with Mr. Langtry in vigilant attendance.' But could such a life of unremitting pleasure last?

6 Still on the Bright Side

THE LANGTRYS' CRISIS, IN FACT, was not to descend upon them for another two years. So Lillie continued to enjoy both the company of her new aristocratic connections and also of that circle of artists and writers who had first welcomed her to London.

These Bohemian friends – most of them still striving to make their mark in the world – not only gave Lillie pleasure by their admiration of her beauty, but, by their talk of painting, sculpture and literature, they appealed to her active mind and helped to develop her taste. This obviously stood her in good stead when she was in the company of such art connoisseurs as Lord Malmesbury, to whose treasure-filled Heron Court in Hampshire the Langtrys were several times invited.

Then there was the occasion when the painter Whistler offered practical help on the Langtrys' moving from Eaton Place to the socially more acceptable Norfolk Street, Park Lane. Lillie, with her usual energy, found the furnishing of this 'hood-winking little abode' delightful. She did, however, readily admit falling a prey to antique dealers, securing 'amazing bargains in artificially worm-eaten and blackened-oak, wherewith to furnish my dining-room'; while the plum coloured material with which she draped her drawing room 'made it look prematurely funereal.'

'To the rescue of this gloomy room came Whistler unexpectedly one morning, bearing bundles of palm-leaf fans and a tin of gold paint … I listened gladly to his suggestions of gilded trophies to brighten the walls. So we set to work to burnish the fans, but the gold paint rained on us, and splashed us with such animate persistence that, by the time our work was finished, our eyelashes glittered, and destruction sat on our clothes. Still, the addition of a painted ceiling, dimly representing the firmament, with a pair of birds (prophetically) depicted in full flight thereon, made the drawing-room at all events original as regards decoration.'

Another member of the group who made a particular effort at this time to influence her taste in all matters artistic was Oscar Wilde. He was just down from Oxford with the Newdigate Prize for his poem 'Ravenna', though he was later to be famous for his plays such as 'The Importance of Being Ernest'. They had first met in 1876 when the twenty-two-year-old Irishman told a friend that he was just off to Frank Miles' Studio to meet 'the loveliest woman in Europe.'

Lillie's description of Wilde was not quite so flattering: 'He had a profusion of brown hair, brushed back from his forehead, and worn rather longer than was conventional, though not with the exaggeration which he afterwards affected. His face was large, and so colourless that a few pale freckles of good size were oddly conspicuous. He had a well-shaped mouth, with somewhat coarse lips and greenish-hued teeth. The plainness of his face, however, was redeemed by the splendour of his great, eager eyes.

In height he was about six feet, and broad in proportion. His hands were large and indolent, with pointed fingers and perfectly shaped filbert nails, indicative of his artistic disposition. The nails, I regretfully record, rarely received the attention they deserved. To me he was always grotesque in appearance, although I have seen him described by a French writer as 'beautiful' and 'Apollo-like'.'

Lillie did, though, acknowledge, 'That he possessed a remarkably fascinating and compelling personality, and what in an actor would be termed wonderful 'stage presence', is beyond question, and there was about him an enthusiasm singularly captivating. He had one of the most alluring voices that I have ever listened to, round and soft, and full of variety and expression, and the cleverness of his remarks received added value from his manner of delivering them.'

By 1879 Wilde had moved into Frank Miles' 'untidy and romantic house' just off the Strand, where he cultivated the habit of having 'beautiful people' to tea. Here Lillie was introduced, among others, to the poet Swinburne; while to Norfolk Street, Wilde brought that celebrated arbiter of taste, John Ruskin, then Slade Professor of Art at Oxford. In Ruskin's presence Lillie initially felt overawed, especially as Wilde was being reverential to the great man. But, 'after a few moments, however, Ruskin's winning voice and charm of manner reassured me and, taking courage to look at him, I noted that his blue-eyes were smiling at me under bushy eyebrows, that his forehead was large and intellectual, that his nose was aquiline, and that the side-whiskers made familiar by his earlier portraits had become supplementary to a grey leonine beard.

His hair was rather long, and floppy over his ears; indeed, he was a shaggy-looking individual. He held forth on his topic – Greek art – in a fervently enthusiastic manner, and, as vehemently denounced the Japanese style, as the 'Glorification of ugliness and artificiality!' Lillie was not to know that later Ruskin would fling one his famous denunciations at her – in public too – calling her a 'Jezebel'.

As well as introducing Lillie to his wide circle of friends, Wilde also willingly undertook her further education. Lillie freely admitted the debt she owed to this 'great student', writing that 'even during the whirl of my first season he induced me to improve my mind by attending Newton's lectures on Greek art at the British Museum, to the manifest delight of the students, who used to gather outside the door to receive us with cheers'.

At first Lillie was also grateful to receive the young poet's homage: 'Before Oscar had achieved celebrity, and was unconsciously on the verge of it, he always made a point of bringing me flowers, but he was not in circumstances to afford great posies, so, in coming to call, he would drop into Covent Garden flower market, buy me a single gorgeous amaryllis (all his slender purse would allow), and stroll down Piccadilly carrying the solitary flower. The scribblers construed his act of homage as a pose, and thus I innocently conferred on him the title 'Apostle of the Lily'. This public gesture was later parodied by Gilbert in 'Patience' – his satire on the whole aesthetic movement of 'Art for Arts Sake' – in the verse:

> *Though the Philistines may jostle*
> *You will rank as an apostle*
> *In the high aesthetic band,*
> *As you walk down Piccadilly*
> *With a poppy or a lily*
> *In your mediaeval hand.*

In recognition of Wilde's generosity, Lillie lent him Poynter's portrait of her, for him to display on an easel in his aesthetically furnished drawing room.

In the early part of their acquaintance, Lillie found Wilde 'really ingenuous. His mannerisms and eccentricities were then but the natural outcome of a young fellow bustling over with temperament, and were not all assumed.' Later their relationship became more intense, and to Lillie, therefore rather ridiculous. 'For instance, one night he curled up to sleep on my doorstop, and Mr. Langtry, returning unusually late, put an end to his poetic dreams by tripping over him.' They began to have tiffs and Lillie did not always have the time to be the serious student, he demanded, as one of her letters to Wilde explains: 'Of course I'm trying to learn more Latin, but we stay here until Wednesday night so I shan't be able to see my kind tutor before Thursday. Do come and see me that afternoon, about six if you can. I called at Salisbury Street about an hour before you left. I wanted to ask you how I should go to a fancy-dress ball there, but I chose a soft black Greek dress with a fringe of silver crescents and stars and diamond ones in my hair and on my neck and called it Queen of Night. I made it myself.

I wanted to write more but this horrid paper and pen prevent me, so when we meet I will tell you more (only don't tell Frank).'

So, despite Wilde presenting Lillie with a white, vellum-bound copy of his poem 'The New Helen' – with its engaging dedication 'To Helen, formerly of Troy, now of London' – she had to admit she had become tired of him. 'There were times when I found him too persistent in hanging round the house or running about after me elsewhere, and I am afraid that often I said things which hurt his feelings in order to get rid of him. After a frank remark I made on one occasion, I happened to go to the theatre, and as I sat in my box, I noticed a commotion in the stalls – it was Oscar, who, having perceived me suddenly, was being led away in tears by his friend Frank Miles.'

The 'Triptych' drawn by Frank Miles

To outward appearances it also seemed that Lillie was as firmly fixed in Royal Circles as she ever was: at Cowes she had been introduced to Princess Alexander's parents, the King and Queen of Denmark; at Marlborough House she had met the future Emperor and Empress (Bertie's sister) of Germany; she had been given signed photographs by both Prince Wilhelm of Glücksburg and the King of Sweden; in September 1879, when Bertie's two sons set off to be midshipmen of HMS *Bacchante*, Lillie bought them both keepsakes. In fact, fifteen-year-old Prince Eddy immediately attached Lillie's gift to his watch chain, confessing artlessly: 'I had to take off my grandmother's [Queen Victoria's] locket to make room for it'. Lillie had also been embarassed during a cotillon in Baron Rothschild's Piccadilly house, by Crown Prince Rudolf of Austria – 'a callow youth', and even been amorously pursued in her own home by Leopold, King of the Belgians.

Many years later, contrasting her own life at this time with that of her two circles of friends, Lillie was to write: 'Looking back on this period, I find a difficulty in placing the exact moment when I felt a changed attitude toward the undreamed-of social maelstrom into which I had been swept. Most of the people with whom I associated were either persons of importance in the land, with duties and responsibilities towards their country, or they were artists working hard to become rich and great, while I was absolutely idle, my only purpose in life being to look nice and make myself agreeable.'

But at the time, Lillie also knew that the Langtrys' financial crisis was creeping closer every day.

7 Another Turn of Fortune's Wheel

DESPITE THESE PLEASANT INTERLUDES IN the two years following Lillie's presentation at Court, it gradually became apparent both to Lillie and her public that her fortunes were changing. To begin with, to continue living in this 'fairyland' cost money, and Lillie started to deplore the spendthrift she had now become: 'For the first time in my life I became intoxicated with the idea of arraying myself as gorgeously as the Queen of Sheba, and being accorded unlimited credit by the dressmakers, who enjoyed designing original 'creations' for me, I began to pile up bills at their establishments, heedless of the day of reckoning that must eventually come....

I shuddered when I remembered that two morning costumes and one evening gown had seemed ample in my unsophisticated days, and that when I was suddenly, so to speak, assimilated by London Society I had been quite unaware of the fact that dress mattered at all. Now I required a new outfit for every occasion, and my husband aiding and abetting me by his approval, I became more and more reckless, allowing insidious saleswomen to line negligées with ermine or border gowns with silver fox without inquiring the cost, until the Christmas bills poured in, laying bare my colossal extravagance.'

Furthermore, this fine style of dressing made unthinkable the hiring of a straw-strewn four-wheeler to get from one stately home to another. So the Langtrys were forced to buy a chestnut horse and brougham, which had to be kept 'in the mews at the back of our doll's-house,' together with the gift of the thoroughbred hack Redskin. Another expense.

By this time, too, Edward Langtry's income from his Irish estates was almost non-existent, as Lillie humorously remembers: 'Roofs fell in; pigs died; farms were inundated, and cottages became uninhabitable with such stubborn persistency that, at last, my husband buckled on his armour and went to the Green Isle to investigate the cause in person. But money seeming scarcer than ever after that rash expedition, I suspected the good-natured happy-go-lucky Irishman of refilling the pigsties and rebuilding the entire village of Parkgate.' She could expect no help from her family in Jersey, nor could she appeal to any of her new friends in London. As for the Prince of Wales, from him she had received several gifts, including the 'Red House' in Bournemouth, but never money.

But there was a noticeable change in her relationship with Bertie too. His attention had been caught by that amazing tragedienne of the Comédie Francaise – Sarah Bernhardt. Oscar Wilde may have been one of the first to greet the French actress when she arrived in Folkstone, but it was Bertie – having already met her on one of his Paris visits – who took a box for the whole of her Company's 1879 London season.

Lillie herself first met Sarah at the breakfast given by Sir Algernon Borthwick to welcome the principal members of the Company. Those of the fashionable set who were also present had the rare sight of two of the most brilliant women of their time seated either side of their host. Lillie's opinion of the 'Divine Sarah' – the title she earned from her English critics for her dazzling performance as the Queen in Victor Hugo's 'Ruy Blas' – was frank: 'This great and overwhelming artist was almost too individual, too exotic, to be completely understood or properly estimated all at once. Her superb diction, her lovely silken voice, her natural acting, her passionate temperament, her fire – in a word, transcendent genius – caused amazement in a day when British acting (with a few notable exceptions) was of the stagey, posturing description.'

The similarity of Sarah's London reception to her own, only three years earlier, cannot have escaped Lillie. She was even made to share in Wilde's fascination for this 'Queen of the Drama' from France. 'Painters and poets admired her. Oscar Wilde enthused over her likeness to coins of the ancient Romans and carried me off to the British Museum to hunt for her profile in coins, intaglios, and vases of the period, in some of which we found almost exact replicas of her symmetrical Latin features. Like all great beauty it did not blaze upon one's vision, but grew upon acquaintance. And hers, being a combination of intelligence, of feature and of soul, remained with her until the end of her life.'

At the Prince of Wales' insistence, Sarah soon became a frequent guest at Marlborough House and, on one occasion, had to miss a rehearsal because she found it impossible to excuse herself from the Prince's company. Sarah's note to her Company's maestro gave the details: 'It is twenty past one. I can't rehearse any more at this hour. The P. has kept me since eleven.'

But Bertie was not the only one of the two, apparently, looking elsewhere for company. Lillie was still writing to the Jersey friend of her youth, Arthur Jones; he still carried her impetuous and passionate letters with him 'in a little green case'. Writing from Norfolk Street she once told him, 'I am so cross at the idea of you not coming back till Monday' and asked him to bring with him when he did come 'a waterproof rug from my stable if there is one.... also a bottle of brilliantine from Hugo hairdresser, 5, Sloane Street – I have a bill there so please don't pay for it.' She concluded by pleading, 'Darling Artie do write and say you Thursday like a good boy – Good-bye, miss me very much. Yr. Loving Lillie.'

There was, too, her relationship with the nineteen-year-old son of the aristocratic Shrewsbury family, whose mother thought that an attachment to a married woman 'would keep him out of mischief' but whose presence in Lillie's drawing room somewhat 'miffed' the Prince of Wales. Yet, at the same time, in public, Lillie liked to prove that the Prince continued to be in her thrall.

This confidence she was soon to find misplaced.

Shortly before Sarah Bernhardt returned to Paris with her Company, she and Lillie were each in charge of a stall at a grand charity fête being held in the Royal Albert Hall. The Prince of Wales was there and first bought an oil painting done by Sarah herself and then moved to Lillie's stall. She was pouring tea at five shillings a cup, or one guinea if she had first taken a sip. Lillie poured Bertie a cup of tea and then, without being asked, put her lips to the rim of the cup. The Prince put his cup down untouched. 'I should like a clean one, please,' he said firmly, afterwards putting two sovereigns into her hand and walking away.

There was another story going the rounds that also suggested that Lillie had gone too far in her familiarity with the Prince: at a fancy-dress ball she was reported to have slipped a piece of ice down his back. Lillie, however, was always to deny the truth of this tale, saying that the real culprit was an audacious Irish beauty – Mrs. Cornwallis West – who 'popped a spoonful of strawberry-ice down her husband's back', because he wanted to leave the party and she was not yet ready to go.

There was worse still to come. So far the affair between Lillie and Bertie had never once been alluded to in the British press. Yet in 1879, when, ironically, the affair was coming to an end, it was brought to public attention in 'Town Talk' by its twenty-seven- year-old editor, Adolphus Rosenberg. In the 30th August edition of the magazine, Rosenberg claimed that, 'A petition has been filed in the Divorce Court by Mr. Edward Langtry, H.R.H. The Prince of Wales, and two other gentlemen whose names up to the time of going to press we have not been enabled to learn, are mentioned as co-respondents.'

Emboldened by the public's fervid interest and the resultant rise in his magazine's circulation, in a later issue Rosenberg went on to point an accusing finger at the lady in the case: 'When we have a lady's name paraded before the public in a thousand different ways, when we see her photographs displayed in almost every stationer's window: when we see that photograph side by side with bishops and lawyers, and in conjunction with facial representation of well-known harlots, the question arises, 'who is Mrs. Langtry?' ' He even went so far as to give the names of the two hitherto unknown correspondents – the Lords Lonsdale and Londesborough.

Suddenly, however, on 4th October, Rosenberg published a surprising retraction: 'I am informed on authority which I have no reason to doubt that Mr. Langtry has withdrawn the petition which he had filed in the Divorce Court. The case of Langtry vs Langtry and others is therefore finally disposed of and we have probably heard the last of it.'

But this, in fact, was not to be the end of the case. Rosenberg, in the same 4th October issue, had rashly attacked Mrs. Cornwallis-West for making thousands of pounds every year on the sale of her photographs. Immediately her husband sued Rosenberg for 'filthy and foul' defamatory libel. What is more, to his great surprise, Rosenberg learned that he was also to be charged, at the same time, for libelling Lillie and Edward Langtry in six separate issues of 'Town Talk'.

The case, which had been made by public interest into a cause célèbre, was heard on 25th October, at London's Central Criminal Court. During the proceedings the Prosecution pointed out that both the Prince and the Princess of Wales had frequently visited the Langtrys' home in Norfolk Street. Furthermore, 'The lady of whom this libel has been published is of great personal attractions and beauty. Hence it has been that the defendant [Rosenberg] and those who are associated with him, have thought fit for the purpose of profit, and for the sake of their vile publication, to make her the subject of obloquy and defamation.'

Lillie herself was not present, so it was left to Edward to assure the court that what Rosenberg had printed was untrue; that he had never thought of divorcing his wife; and that he had 'always lived on terms of affection' with her. Rosenberg was sentenced to eighteen months in prison, with the judge regretting that he could not add 'hard labour'.

8 Prince Louis of Battenberg

DURING THE YEAR FOLLOWING THE trial, Lillie formed a close relationship with a second member of the Royal Family – Prince Louis of Battenberg. Born in Austria, the twenty-six-year-old Prince was one of Bertie's distant cousins and former aide-de-camps and always called him 'Uncle'. Bertie, for his part, thought Louis such 'a remarkably nice boy' that he kept a special room in Marlborough House for his own personal use.

The young Prince's first love was the British Navy and in order to join it he had become a British citizen. But the twenty-six-year- old also enjoyed dancing, swimming, riding and playing the piano, besides being an Honorary Member of the Institute of Painters in Water Colours. His charm and gentle manners made him everybody's favourite, 'especially the ladies'. It was inevitable that he and Lillie should meet when Bertie made him a ship's officer on his yacht *Osborne*.

1880, however, was also the year when Lillie's fortunes fell to their nadir. From Jersey came the news of her father's disgrace. He had been asked to leave Jersey because the Diocesan authorities could no longer turn a blind eye to his numerous 'amours'. Though William Le Breton was listed in *Crockfords* as the Dean of Jersey until his death, he was in fact demoted and sent back to London to be a Vicar in Marylebone.

Then, once it was seen that the Prince of Wales had begun to withdraw his favours from Lillie, not only did society start to turn its back on her, but the Langtrys' creditors took this as their cue to withdraw their credit. As a result, in October, Edward was declared bankrupt.

In the midst of all this, Lillie suspected that she was pregnant with Prince Louis' child. In her panic, she immediately contacted her confidante in Jersey, her 'own darling', Arthur Jones. 'I am not yet ... I am sure there must be something wrong or what I took would have made me. Please go to a chemist and ask how many doses one ought to take a day as I must go on taking it.' Once she knew for certain that 'it' had had no effect and she was indeed pregnant, she also knew that there was no chance of her ever becoming Louis' wife. Indeed, Louis' royal connections saw to it that he was immediately sent back to serve in the Navy.

In November, the financial crisis came: 'Bailiffs invaded the little Norfolk Street house, and Mr. Langtry frequently found it convenient to go fishing, leaving me to deal with the unwelcome intruders as best I could.

The same faithful maid, an Italian named Dominique, had been with me all through my astonishing London experiences. This devoted woman took the matter of the bailiffs' sojourn much more keenly to heart than I did, and during this harassing time she never missed an opportunity of cramming my few trinkets and other treasured trifles and, indeed, anything portable, into the pockets of anyone who came to visit me. In this way some very distinguished friends departed from the beleaguered house with their pockets full, all unconscious that they were evading the law.'

All the Langtrys' household effects then had to be sold to pay their creditors. Lillie herself was not at the auction, so Lady Lonsdale wrote to tell her what had happened: 'Everything went for immense prices your little tea-table with your initials on down to your skates – so I hope your horrid creditors are satisfied.'

So what was Lillie to do now? She had nowhere to live and Louis' baby was expected the following Spring. The only solution open to her was to wait for the birth in Jersey, where her mother would be able to look after her. To keep her secret from Edward, she suggested he go on an American trip. Edward later recalled,

'I was packed off to America on some business which kept me dodging about Chicago and New York.' Lillie herself travelled to Jersey with Dominique, where she rented a small cottage on the outskirts of St. Helier. Even the Press did not know the true story – the *New York Times* simply stated: 'Mr. and Mrs. Langtry have given up their London residence, and for the present Mrs. Langtry remains in Jersey,' and continued with welcome words of praise for Lillie: 'Is beauty deposed, or has beauty abdicated? The result on London society will be the same. Public pets may be objectionable, but few could so well have survived the ordeal of public admiration and reserved so much of the natural good hearted woman as Mrs. Langtry.'

There was, however, no way in which Lillie could keep the birth of a baby secret in so small a place as Jersey. So it was arranged from London that she should travel incognito to Paris. There she was to stay in an apartment belonging to one of Bertie's personal friends. According to Mary Malcolm, Lillie's grand-daughter, being interviewed in 1978 about her mother's birth: 'Two men from Buckingham Palace accompanied her. The secrecy surrounding my mother's birth was quite extraordinary. In the weeks leading up to the confinement Lillie led a wretched life hidden away in Paris, not allowed out except for short journeys in a close carriage, and always wearing a double veil ... While she was in Paris, elaborate arrangements were made for her letters to be posted to him [Edward] from Jersey so as to make it seem she was merely visiting her parents.'

Even more extraordinary than the circumstances of Lillie's waiting for the birth of her baby was the Prince of Wales' involvement in the secrecy. It was just one more example of Bertie's readiness to stand by his friends when they were in need. However, though Lillie may have been contrasting her present Parisian stay, at the Hôtel Castille, with a previous secret visit with Bertie himself at the Hôtel Bristol, it was Arthur Jones that Lillie now wanted to be with her. On 9th December 1880 a telegram from Paris was delivered to him at the Victoria Club in

St. Helier begging: 'Do come not ill but so miserable.' In a letter she wrote: 'Ah you must some soon, be a good little boy and let yr farm as you proposed'; in another Lillie suggests the strength of the bond that she feels exists between them: 'I have always you at all events haven't I? to care for me whatever happens.'

Jeanne-Marie was born in Paris in March 1881. Lillie returned to Jersey with her, now seemingly ready to substitute the role of mother for the life of a Professional Beauty and the beloved of two Royal Princes. In a word, ready once more to become a real 'Jersey Lily.'

9 Lillie back to Centre Stage

DID LILLIE LANGTRY REALLY STAY in Jersey for the rest of her life? Here is her story of what happened next: 'Being young and of optimistic tendency, my nature quickly rebounded from the shock of misfortune, and I soon ceased to take our financial tumble greatly to heart, and presently returned to London, where I took a quiet apartment. Shepherded by my faithful, white-haired Dominique, who daily gave further proof of her devotion, and appeared to have unlimited resources at her command, I had not been permitted to feel any acute need of money, although I saw little or nothing of Mr. Langtry, who now fished perpetually.'

Lillie's grand-daughter's account fills in the details that Lillie herself preferred to omit: 'Very soon after my mother was born, Lillie moved back to London to take up life as though nothing had happened, and the baby – Jeanne Marie – was moved to a small house in Bournemouth, built by Edward VII, where she was looked after by Lillie's mother. Until she was thirteen or fourteen Jeanne Marie was ignorant of the fact that Lillie Langtry, the King's mistress, was her mother. She called her 'ma tante' (my aunt) – she was brought up to speak French as a first language – and even after she learned the truth she still believed her father was Edward Langtry.' When she was very young, she had even been told that Maurice, who had died in India, was her father.

Though Lillie was by now convinced 'how little money is needed to keep body and soul together,' she nevertheless had to have some income and it was clear that she would have no financial support from Edward, Bertie or Louis. So her friends came up with ideas of how she could earn her own living: Frank Miles – himself a keen gardener – suggested horticulture; Whistler thought she could become an artist; it was Oscar Wilde, though, who thought she should become an actress and who brought her to the attention of the wife of M.P. Henry Labouchere – the actress Henrietta Hodson.

'I should like to print her name in capitals of gratitude,' Lillie was to write later, 'for she determined my future through her sheer pertinacity, and launched me on a career of pleasurable striving after the unattainable.' Henrietta's first move was to call on Lillie in her modest flat in 18 Albert Mansions, Victoria Street, where apparently, 'She plunged at once into the subject of her visit. A rumour that I was studying for the stage was her excuse for coming to ask me to take part in a semi-private amateur entertainment being organised by her for some local charity at the Town Hall, Twickenham.'

Next, Henrietta took Lillie off to her villa on the River Thames to coach her as Lady Clara in the twenty-minute one-act play in which she herself was to play the other part. Here Lillie soon found that being an actress was not nearly as easy as being a Professional Beauty: 'Learning words was easy enough, but finding the right inflection was such a constant worry that I began to wonder if it could be my native language I was engaged in speaking, so difficult did it seem to me at first to 'get behind' the meaning and phrasing of the 'someone else' who had written the little curtain-raiser.'

On 19th November, 1881, for its single charity performance, 'A Fair Encounter' opened at Twickenham Town Hall. But the lively battle of wits between the two women that the play was supposed to be never actually happened: 'When I found myself on the diminutive stage, my mind became a blank. Alas, not a word of the opening soliloquy could I remember. There I stood, a forced smile on my lips and a bunch of roses in my arms, without the vestige of an idea of what was to happen next. Fortunately, after several promptings from my coach, who was listening anxiously for her cue behind the door, I recovered my wits and my words, and the 'encounter' proceeded to a languid finish without further incident.' Lillie had, though, evidently remembered enough of her part for the *The World* to report on her 'full, round and vibrant' voice.

After that nerve-racking experience, Lillie was absolutely determined never to appear on stage again. But she reckoned without Henrietta's powers of persuasion – Lillie's next role was to be Kate Hardcastle in Goldsmith's 'She Stoops to Conquer'. The performance was to be a matinée at the Haymarket Theatre; the other parts were to be taken by leading London actors and actresses, with the charity this time being the Royal General Theatrical Fund.

'As soon as the public announcement was made of the matinée there was a mixed feeling among my friends and relations, and none of them received the new departure with pleasurable anticipation, the one predominating reason being that the conditions of the theatre were not so well understood then as now. But, on realising that I was determined, or, as I alone knew, Henrietta was, they became eager to see how I should acquit myself in my difficult task and there was a rush to book seats. When the day arrived, crowds waited for many hours outside the pit and gallery doors for the opening time, buoyed up with sandwiches and other refreshments, while those blessed with extra foresight had come provided also with camp-stools.'

This was a return to the popularity Lillie had enjoyed during her first London season. There was no disguising the triumph she felt: 'And what an audience it was! Packed with the rank and file of London. The Prince and Princess of Wales were in the royal box, and in the opposite one sat the Duchess of Manchester and a large party. My best friends, too, with their attendant swains, were anxious to get as near as possible, and crowded into the front rows of the stalls, all more or less tittering and amused, and not at all inclined to take me seriously.' Yet, happily, 'the afternoon passed without a hitch; countless bouquets were thrown to me and everything seemed like a dream when it was all over.'

This 'dream', however, had an even more amazing sequel. The Bancrofts, who owned the Haymarket Theatre, asked Lillie to become a member of their own theatrical company. After all, *The Times* had reported of Lillie in the part of Kate Hardcastle:

> Even those who came only to look will admit they had their own money's worth. Exquisite purity of complexion (remarkable in this lady) unaided by art is apt to become paleness on the stage; the brightest of eyes is not seen to advantage across the footlights, but the finely shaped head, the classic profile, the winning smile, the musical laugh, the grace of the figure – 'a full, flowing roundness inclining to length: – these are the gifts which the public in a theatre can appreciate as well as the privileged admirers in a drawing-room, and the enthusiastic applause which greeted Mrs. Langtry on her entrance must be regarded as the willing, eager homage to the far-famed beauty, as well as cordial welcome to the 'débutante'.
>
> The audience evidently came prepared to make every possible allowance, but none whatever was required so far as she was concerned. The oldest playgoers, who had seen half a dozen Miss Hardcastles, were astonished at the ease with which she glided into the part, the accuracy of the conception, and the felicity of the execution throughout. She was good in all, but the test scene is the one in which she plays the barmaid, and here she assumed the pert tone and the required degree of flippancy without once approximating to vulgarity.

So, after spending Christmas with her father at his Marylebone vicarage and agreeing for the sum of £132 (her weight in lbs) to give her name to a full page advertisement in *The Illustrated London News* for Pears Soap, Lillie began the hard work of becoming a professional actress. There were all the dreary

rehearsals in cold, dark theatres, the 'so many trifling but exasperating rules and regulations'. She was certainly never stage-struck: 'I had loomed so largely in the public eye that there was no novelty in facing the crowded audience, in which I knew most of the occupants of the stalls and boxes, and all in the cheaper parts knew me.' In fact, at this early stage in her new career, Lillie even went so far as to deplore 'the urgent need of money that had obliged me to abandon my previous mode of life, which, now that it was over, seemed so desirable and afforded me many pleasant recollections.'

There was, too, a distinct disadvantage in the 1880s in becoming a professional actress: people in high society who warmly applauded those they saw acting in London's fashionable theatres were certainly not willing to give them a warm welcome to their own drawing rooms. For Lillie, who had been a popular guest of the most important families in the country, this was a most unpalatable fact for her to accept. So she planned to circumvent the social barriers that now seemed set up against her. She would win one of the the most outstanding men of his time to her side – William Gladstone, leader of the Liberal Party and Prime

Minister for the second time.

The two had first met briefly at Millais' studio, but Gladstone now became a frequent visitor to Lillie's home. He often shared her pre-theatre dinner; sometimes entertained her by reading aloud his favourite passages from Shakespeare; lent her books and discussed literature with her; even interested himself in her financial affairs; but, most importantly, he gave her a piece of advice that she never forgot and always followed: 'In your professional career, you will receive attacks, personal and critical, just and unjust. Bear them, never reply, and, above all, never rush into print to explain or defend yourself.'

Reflecting afterwards on the effect of this unusual friendship with a powerful politician six years older than her father, Lillie wrote: 'How wonderful it seemed that this great and universally sought-after man should give me and my work even a passing thought. But he did more. His comprehensive mind and sweet nature grasped the difficult task that lay before me, the widely different orbit in which my life would henceforth move, and he knew how adrift I felt. And out of his vast knowledge of the public he realised how much he could help me – so the salmon advised the minnow. Never shall I forget the wisdom of Gladstone and the uplifting effects of his visits.' He was, too, exactly the right person to give Lillie the respectability she needed to continue to be invited to the homes of those she had first met in her London seasons in the late 1870s.

Once the engagements with the Bancrofts had come to an end, Henrietta Labouchère decided that Lillie was now ready to tour the provinces – with her own company. This plan had a definite appeal for Lillie: 'To be my own manager, my own mistress, and free from unaccustomed control changed my point of view entirely.' For Lillie now realised that, though 'my nose was kept to the grindstone,' she was becoming much more interested in the stage and her progress as an actress than she had been. To begin with the four plays she decided to take on tour were 'She Stoops to Conquer'; 'Ours'; 'Peril' and 'As You Like

It' in which she herself took the part of Rosalind.

Manchester, 'the critical city,' acclaimed Lillie deliriously, with students unharnessing the horses and dragging her carriage through the streets; after a week of 'hectic excitement' at Edinburgh, a torchlight procession of students escorted her back to Caledonian Station; in Glasgow she was made much of by the coterie of painters and litterateurs there; Dublin provided 'unusually gay and boisterous audiences; in Belfast, Edward's birthplace, the audience lowered pheasants, hares, and other delicacies from the gallery to the stage to testify their approval of my artistic efforts and insisted on my receiving them at all sorts of dramatic moments.'

For the indefatigable Henrietta even all this adulation was not enough. Her next plan – with the co-operation of the leading American impresario Henry E. Abbey – was to arrange for Lillie and her company to tour the United States, starting with New York. To begin with, Henry Abbey proposed that Lillie's percentage of the tour receipts should be the same as Sarah Bernhardt's whose tours he also organised, but Lillie still retained her Jersey instinct for a good deal and asked for more.

In the end Abbey agreed and offered Lillie a figure higher than any other actress had ever been offered for such an engagement. These advantageous terms allowed Lillie to keep on paying Edward a monthly salary which he had pestered her to do while she was at the Haymarket Theatre. No wonder she wrote ruefully to Arthur Jones in Jersey, 'My darling boy, I wish we were married ....I do so want to get rid of Ned.' Also, before she left England, Lillie let the 'Red House' in Bournemouth and rented a cottage in Jersey where her mother and Dominique could continue to look after eighteen-month-old Jeanne-Marie.

The practical details may have been settled, but Lillie confessed that she was not 'wildly enthusiastic' over the prospect of her American tour. After all, if, compared to Jersey, 'England, to my limited vision, seemed a large slice of the world' it is not surprising that 'the States, at that time, seemed to me to be about as far off as Mars, and nearly as inaccessible.' Then there was the depres-sion she felt at leaving behind her many friends and relations. But Henrietta's determination was not to be thwarted, and Lillie left for America on the *Arizona*, on the 14th October 1882, 'feeling perfectly miserable'.

10 America – the Promised Land

'I HEARD THE FURIOUS BRAYING of a particularly brazen band. I hurried on deck and there found a tug alongside, with Henry E. Abbey and his partner Schoeffel, marshalling a perfect army of reporters, while Oscar Wilde, torn from his slumbers at an unearthly hour, still had the spirit to wave a bunch of lilies in welcome' – Lillie had arrived in New York.

The play Henrietta had chosen for Lillie to make her American début was Tom Taylor's 'An Unequal Match' – a comedy in which Lillie was to play the part of Hester Grazebrook, the illiterate milk-maid who enters polite society as the wife of an English baronet. Henry Abbey was so successful with publicity for the play, that for the first night alone, he had the boxes and stalls auctioned for a total of twenty thousand dollars.

Then disaster struck – or seemed to. On the evening of the first night that Lillie was to appear in the Abbey Park Theatre it caught fire: 'From my window I could see the building, on which all my hopes were centred, with flames bursting through the roof. A great crowd filled Broadway, their attention divided between me and the blazing pile, the light from which illuminated the whole of Madison Square. The only thing that seemed likely to escape the flames was a large board on iron standards high above the roof, with my name – 'Mrs. Langtry' – upon it. I stood intently watching that sign, with a mixed feeling that my fate depended upon its escape from destruction. If it stands, I shall succeed! I cried, 'And,' as it toppled, 'if it burns, I will succeed without it! But it stood!!!' The performance was postponed for a week and then transferred to the Wallack Theatre.

So Lillie trod the American stage for the first time in November 1882 and the box office receipts reached a record seven thousand dollars. Of her performance Oscar Wilde reported: 'It is only in the best Greek gems, on the silver coins of Syracuse, or among the marble fringes of the Parthenon frieze that one can find the ideal representation of the marvellous beauty of that face which laughed through the leaves last night as Hester Grazebrook.' Less kind critics dismissed her as no more than 'a clever attractive amateur.' Lillie herself recalled, 'The evening was memorable, the audience enthusiastic, and the floral tributes showered on me were a revelation.'

It was not long before Lillie – who had originally dreaded leaving England for 'unknown lands' – had to admit 'America grows on me.' For a start, she revelled in 'the immensity of the continent; the excitement of being whirled over vast tracts of magnificent country from one great city to another; the novelty and comfort of railway travelling, and, above all, the warmheartedness of the American welcome made a strong appeal, and so it came to pass that without losing my love for the Union Jack, I coupled with it a great affection for the Stars and Stripes.' Even more important, Dion Boucicault – her new theatrical advisor now Henrietta had returned to England ('somewhat peevishly') – pointed out that 'purely from an actor's point of view, America is the promised land.'

The result was that Lillie and her company had tours in America for five consecutive years and she could boast: 'I can hardly put my finger on any town sufficiently important to be marked on the map in which I have not played more than once.' The plays she put on included both Shakespeare and contemporary drama, with the most popular being 'Macbeth' and the modern play, 'As in a Looking Glass'. Her 'co-worker', as she called him, was Charles Coghan, who not only acted but was the author of several successful plays.

A Boston reporter, having interviewed Lillie in her dressing

room, gives a fascinating glimpse of her behind stage while on
tour:

> Mrs. Langtry insists upon having each dressing-room
> arranged, as to furniture, etc., as nearly alike as possible. This
> is one of the first things her stage-manager, attends to on reaching
> a city. Most of the paraphernalia is carried by Mrs. Langtry when
> on tour. Her dressing-table is of white wood, heavily enamelled
> in white. The table is elaborately ornamented with cupids and
> butterflies, delicately made and grouped and is festooned with
> old rose satin with muslin beneath, peeping through at the top.
> The mirror is electric-lighted to Mrs. Langtry's own special design
> and by an ingenious arrangement, colour effects, blue, red and
> amber, can be obtained at will. Thus the actress, when dressing,
> can always tell just how new gowns, hats, etc., are going to look
> as to the blending of colour when she is on the stage.
>
> For the reception of the very numerous accessories of the
> toilette there is a sort of tray. Nearly everything on this table is
> of gold. Each brush, comb, scent-bottle, powder-box and the like
> is engraved with Mrs. Langtry's initials, the monograms being
> surrounded by a ring of turquoises. The wonderful cases of
> manicure instruments are all fitted with implements of solid gold.
> A cosy sofa of luxurious proportions, decked with alluring
> cushions of daintiest design, and a decidedly business-like, yet
> elegant, escritoire are also included in the equipment of the
> Jersey Lily's dressing-room. The remainder of the room is quite
> in keeping with the things described and it is needless to say the
> general effect is truly magnificent.

During the years of her American tours in the 1880s, Lillie
not only sometimes took time off to visit her mother and Jeanne-
Marie in Jersey, but, on 1st July, 1883, surprised everyone by
enrolling for three months at the Conservatoire of François
Regnier, the leading drama teacher at that period. While Lillie
was there – working from eight in the morning till late at night

– both Sarah Bernhardt and her fellow actor Coquelin were so impressed by Lillie's determination to improve her acting technique, that they volunteered to come to the Conservatoire too, so that they could play opposite her in any of the theatrical excerpts Regnier chose for her. After having the experience of actually acting with Sarah, Lillie wrote, 'I despair of becoming a real actress when I work on the stage with her, and I would gladly exchange my beauty such as it is, for a soupcon of her great talent.'

Nevertheless, for Lillie 'The Play' was never the only thing in her life. She still needed and attracted many friends. These included Freddie Gebhard from Baltimore who had inherited a vast fortune from his father. This tall, dark, athletic-looking twenty-two-year-old, who loved swimming, tennis , riding and sailing, soon became the devoted follower of the twenty-nine-year-old Lillie. He took her ice-skating; travelled on tour with her as what she termed her 'body-guard'; and showed his affection for her by giving her extremely expensive gifts, including a diamond necklace and bracelet from Tiffany's. In 1886 the couple had a three-month tour of the Continent, when they were received by most of the crowned heads of Europe. On their return Freddie bought her a town house in New York. Neither America nor Henrietta Labouchère approved their close relationship, but the scandal of it certainly boosted box office receipts.

Opinions differ as to whether Freddie himself contributed to the one million dollar cost of Lillie's own personal railway carriage, but he was certainly the one who introduced her to Colonel Mann – the inventor of the American equivalent of the Pullman sleeper – who built it for her. As Lillie remembered it: 'I think the Colonel thoroughly enjoyed planning that car. Being very hard at work rehearsing a new play, I let him have his head, and, beyond an occasional letter with reference to colour or material, he did not disturb me with details, so that, when the finished car and the bill burst on my view simultaneously I am not sure whether joy at the possession of such a beautiful perambulating home or horror at my extravagance in ordering it was uppermost in my mind.' Recalling the name of the first horse she and her brother Reggie had bought from the Jersey cattle market when she was fourteen, Lillie christened this carriage that was 'a bliss to me through numerous tours.' Flirt too, but in its Indian translation of 'Lalee'.

The 'Lalee' was seventy-five foot long, blue – Lillie's favourite colour – with a white roof and had platforms made of teak brought specially from India. Lillie's own sleeping quarters were upholstered in Nile-green silk brocade and absolutely everything, even her dressing table, was padded – just in case the train should be involved in an accident. In the cream and green brocaded saloon Lillie was delighted to find a piano; the kitchen was sufficiently equipped to serve full-course dinners; while running underneath the length of the train were enormous ice-chests, capable, Lillie noted of 'housing a whole stag', which they did on one occasion. Perhaps the youngest guest to be invited on board to enjoy all these luxuries was Lillie's 'niece', Jeanne-Marie, during her visits to America with Lillie's mother and her governess.

As Lillie herself recorded, 'Money came in very freely during my tours in the United States, therefore I looked about in New York and elsewhere for suitable investments, and decided to place a considerable part of my earnings in land, when I should find something I fancied.' So when she toured the Pacific coast during her second American season, she bought a six-thousand-acre ranch in Lake Country, in the Californian Howell Mountains. The key word of that ranch was 'Liberty', both for those who worked on it and for Lillie herself, who liked nothing better than being 'up at daybreak and off immediately after breakfast, dressed in cow-boy style, with shirt and breeches, and long mocassins as a protection from rattlesnakes and so forth, galloping about on a cowpony exploring every corner of the land.' There was, too, a tame fawn which wandered round the ranch house, and Lillie several times found it lying on her bed, with its forelegs affectionately round her cat's neck.

Unfortunately, though, the ranch's overseer, despite being 'a good fellow' and meaning to do things 'for the best', happened to have more enthusiasm than common-sense about horses and racing. None of his plans to breed horses and race them on Lillie's behalf succeeded and after several of the expensive thoroughbred mares he had bought for her were either maimed or killed in a terrible railway accident, the disheartened Lillie never visited the ranch again. After owning the property for several more years, Lillie was, in the end, glad to sell it for about half the price she gave for it.

A much happier American experience came about all because a certain Roy Bean, who in 1885 had been elected Justice of the Peace of the South Texan town of Vinagaroon, happened, while visiting Chicago, to see Lillie on stage. He was so captivated by her beauty that as soon as he got back to Val Verde County he renamed his small town 'Langtry'. He then wrote to Lillie asking her to honour Langtry with a visit. Lillie was, unfortunately, too busy to accept, so, 'on writing my regrets, I offered to present an ornamental drinking fountain as a sop; but Roy Bean's quick reply was that it would be quite useless, as the only thing the citizens of Langtry did not drink was water.'

Jersey Lilly Saloon

Several years later, in 1904, Lillie received a second invitation to visit Langtry. This time she was free to attend. The Southern Pacific Railway too was willing to hold the train at the station for half an hour: 'So my company and I awaited the new experience all agog, working ourselves up to the high point of interest and anticipation as the train, having crossed the Pecos river, sped nearer and nearer my town.' Then, in what still appeared to be the middle of a parched sandy plain covered in sage brush and low-growing cactus, the train came to a sudden stop.

'I hurriedly alighted, just as a cloud of sand heralded the approach of a numerous throng of citizens ploughing their way along the entire length of the train to give me the 'glad hand'. That the order of procedure had been thought out and organised was soon evident, for at the head of the ceremonious procession were the officials of the little Texas town, who received me very heartily.

Justice of the Peace Dodd, a quiet, interesting man, introduced himself, and then presented Postmaster Fielding, Stationmaster Smith, and other people of consequence. Next in order came a number of cowboys, who were also formally introduced. Langtry did not boast a newspaper, and therefore these young men had been gathered in from the ranges by means of mounted messengers.

They were all garbed in their finest leathers and most flamboyant shirts (as became the occasion), making a picturesque group, one loosing off his his gun as he passed me in tangible proof of his appreciation of my visit.

Thirty or forty girls, all about fifteen or sixteen, followed and were announced en bloc as 'the young ladies of Langtry'. And finally, 'our wives' brought up the rear. Justice Dodd then welcomed me in apt speech, and, after recounting the history of the town from its inception, declared that it would have been the proudest day in the late 'King' Bean's life (he had been dead only a few months) if he had lived to meet me, adding with obvious embarrassment, that his eldest son, aged twenty-one, who had been cast for the leading role in this unique reception, had received a sudden summons to San Francisco on important business. But it was generally whispered that he had taken flight at the prospect of the responsible part he was to play, and was lying in hiding somewhere among the universal sage-brush.'

The town centre was too far away for Lillie to go and see, but she did have time to step inside the nearby Saloon bar which had been named, though mispelled, the 'Jersey Lilly' after her. It consisted of 'a long, narrow room, which comprised the entire ground floor, whence a ladder staircase led to a sleeping-loft. One side of the room was given up to a bar, naturally the most important feature of the place – while stoutly-made tables and a few benches occupied the vacant space. The tables showed plainly that they had been severely used, for they were slashed as if with bowie-knives, and on each was a well-thumbed deck of playing cards. It was here that Roy Bean, Justice of the Peace, and self-styled 'law west of the Pecos River', used to hold his court and administer justice which, incidentally, sometimes brought 'grist to the mill'. The stories I was told of his ready wit and audacity made me indeed sorry that he had not lived over my visit.'

But that was not all that Langtry had to offer Lillie. The 'Lalee' was already the home of several pets such as a jumping frog from Charleston, an alligator from Florida, plus a tame prairie dog called Bob, so the citizens of Langtry wanted to add one more – 'a huge cinnamon bear', a pet of the late Roy Bean. Fortunately for Lillie, while attempts were being made to hoist the bear on to the train, he broke loose. In his stead, Lillie was presented with the Judge's revolver, which carried the following inscription: 'Presented by W.D.Dodd, of Langtry, Texas, to Mrs. Lillie Langtry in honour of her visit to our town. This pistol was formerly the property of Judge Roy Bean. It aided him in finding some of his famous decisions and keeping order west of the Pecos River. It also kept order in the Jersey Lilly Saloon. Kindly accept this as a small token of our regards.'

~

As well as America allowing Lillie all her theatrical successes, a chance to invest money, and a peep inside a Saloon bar called after a flower from her native island, it also allowed Lillie to change her status twice. She decided to divorce Edward. But first she had to become an American citizen. So, after July 1887, the American Lillie Langtry was able to have her marriage to Edward dissolved in Lake Port, California. The grounds? Edward had deserted her. A year later, when Lillie, now one of the world's wealthiest women in her own right, was on tour in Chicago, she had news of her father. Still nominally the Dean of Jersey, William Le Breton had died alone in Kennington, South London, with just £5 to his name.

11 Mr. Jersey at the Races

THE 'ILL-OMEN' OF LOSING so many of her horses in the railway accident not only dissuaded Lillie from ever going back to her Californian ranch, but it also persuaded her to return to England immediately. From then on, she only visited America – 'to fill engagements'. Determined now to have her permanent base in London, she eventually bought a house in Pont Street, Belgravia, to which all her furniture, horses and carriages were transported from America. From here she continued her acting career, leased theatres, toured the provinces and even agreed to appear on stage in Jersey. But she refused to appear in Oscar Wilde's 'Lady Windermere's Fan' – ironically the story of a society woman and her illegitimate daughter – which he had written especially for her, saying she was far too young for the part.

One of Lillie's first moves was to take a two year lease of St. James Theatre which opened with 'As You Like It'. But she called it her 'unlucky theatre', when she lost money having to cancel performances on contracting first measles and then pleurisy. However, when the theatre did finally open in November 1889 with 'As You Like It', seats were sold out for four months. *The Times* noted, 'Mrs. Langtry is a bewitching Rosalind. The improvement in her acting is astounding.' Then, when she wanted to produce 'Anthony and Cleopatra' – with spectacular effects – the St. James' stage was too small, so in 1891 she also had to lease the larger Prince's Theatre. The expenses incurred running these two theatres made her at the end of one week quite unable to pay the carpenters still busy making the architectural scenery, purple galleys and Roman chariots for the new production. In desperation she sent a messenger to the wealthy Alfred Rothschild, pleading for a temporary loan until she could cable her American bank for funds. It was all worth it, for the *Telegraph* praised her as the 'finest Cleopatra of our time' and the first night audience had her back for fourteen curtain calls.

Lillie as Cleopatra at the Prince's Theatre, 1890

Lillie was the first, though, to see the funny side of her mishaps. On the first night of 'Linda Gray' at the Prince's Theatre, which was attended by the Prince of Wales and his royal party, she recorded that 'the chimney in the royal room smoked H.R.H. and Prince Christian out of it, and that they spent most of the evening on the stage, very busy helping us with our lines, of which we were none of us too sure; also that Bernard Gould (Bernard Partridge) wore an opulent false moustache, which dropped off in the love scene.'

It was typical of Lillie too that, despite these setbacks, she found something new to entertain her. She provided herself with a roulette wheel and cloth, limited the money placed to shillings, so that, without danger to their pockets, she and her guests could enjoy her miniature casino at her after-theatre supper parties.

From her Union Bank in Sloane Square, though, Lillie lost a great deal more than shillings. An ingenious thief forged her signature from her Pear's soap advertisement to authorise the removal of her jewellery box from the Bank's safe. There was a ransom note asking for £5,000 for the jewellery's return, which the Bank grudgingly advanced, but the jewellery was never returned, so Lillie sued the Bank for negligence and finally agreed to settle out of court for £10,000.

An invitation for Lillie to appear in Jersey had been given as early as 1889, but she had always been too busy to accept until one day she unexpectedly sent the theatre management a telegram: 'Will Jersey people like to see me?' Within a fortnight Lillie had organised her company to bring over 'As You Like It', with herself as Rosalind, for two performances at the Theatre Royal in Gloucester Street, where the Opera House now stands. And did Lillie's fellow Islanders like to see her? *The Jersey Times* and *British Press* of April 30th 1891 reported their reception:

Naturally, great curiosity was aroused to see how the lady, who claims Jersey as the island of her birth, and in whom therefore Jersey people take an exceptional interest, comported herself as an actress upon the stage....The doors of the theatre were besieged for an hour and an half before the announced opening time, (7.30), by a crowd of people, and many were unable to gain admittance. In honour of the occasion a line of bunting was suspended from the roof of the theatre to the opposite side of the street, and in the neighbourhood flags were flying. At the box entrance a large crowd assembled on each side of the portico to witness the arrivals, and as carriage after carriage deposited its occupants in evening dress at the doors, the costumes of the ladies were inspected with eager interest by the members of the gentler sex. Several policemen in uniform were on duty in front of the theatre, but beyond directing the traffic, their services were not required, the crowd behaving itself in the most orderly fashion. When Mrs. Langtry arrived in her carriage only a few recognised her, but the greeting of her friends was heartily taken up by the general spectators, and she gracefully bowed her acknowledgements.

And Lillie's performance as Rosalind? ...

Mrs. Langtry was, of course, the pivot of attention. It is not the custom, as a rule, for great artistes to surround themselves with a brilliant galaxy of talent lest their own light should be submerged, but speaking generally, Mrs. Langtry had a very judiciously selected company... Mrs. Langtry was received with a loud outburst of applause when she appeared in the second scene of the first act, attired in a magnificent costume, principally composed of lavender-coloured silk. Her fame is now world-wide and we may state that she acted all through with a smoothness and consistency which showed her to be a talented, experienced and altogether superior actress. She was seen to most advantage in the Arden Forest scene, when, accompanied by the faithful Celia she discovered the love messages left by Orlando.

When Jersey's Lieutenant Governor, General C.B. Ewart, knew of Lillie's Jersey engagement, he invited her to appear on the third night in a special command performance of 'The Lady of Lyons'. Both Islanders and *The Jersey Times* were even more enthusiastic in their praise:

As on the two previous evenings, the interior of the Theatre presented a brilliant and animated spectacle; and for the second time the performance was honoured by the presence of His Excellency, the Lt. Governor. The officers of the South Lancashire

Regiment were also present in strong force, their scarlet uniforms adding warmth of colour to a picture already bright and varied with the rich hues of the ladies' costumes ... Opinions may differ as to the suitability or otherwise of some of the more recent impersonations undertaken by Mrs. Langtry during her remarkable theatrical career, but it seems agreed on all hands that in the character of the haughty imperious beauty of Lyons who, with all her exalted notions of the aristocracy finds herself married, not to the prince she thought, but to a gardener's son, has found a part which might have been specially conceived and written for her. When she first made her appearance she was received with applause if anything more hearty and continuous than that which greeted her on the two previous evenings, and as she stood in the centre of the stage gracefully bowing her acknowledgements, a loud cheer broke from the admiring spectators, and it was a minute or so before the performance could be resumed.

Acting, however, was 'temporarily abandoned', as Lillie put it, when she returned to her old love of racing and instantly became totally absorbed in it. In her youth there had been the annual Jersey Races on Gorey Common, then the frequent race-going with the Prince of Wales in the 1870s. Now, though, Lillie was able to be more than a mere race-goer – she could become a horse-owner and breeder.

It all came about through her close friendship with George Alexander Baird, a wealthy, eccentric, and extremely hot-tempered Scotsman, who rode his own horses under the pseudonym of 'Squire Abingdon'. In 1892, after Lillie had visited her mother and Jeanne-Marie in Jersey while Baird was stag-hunting in Scotland, she decided to go to Worth's in Paris for some more new gowns. While in her Paris hotel, she happened to meet the wealthy young Robert Peel. The suspicious Baird, once he discovered that Lillie had gone to Paris instead of returning to London, pursued her there and – after a bout of heavy drinking – went round to her hotel. He found Lillie entertaining Peel in her private suite.

In his jealous and drunken fury, Baird first gave Peel a violent thrashing. Then he turned on Lillie. He hit her so hard that he blacked both her eyes and knocked her unconscious. Then he smashed everything in sight and ripped her new Worth gowns to shreds. Lillie was rushed to hospital, where she had to stay ten days to recover. Baird was arrested and jailed on the charge that Lillie signed against him.

The White Ladye.

Then the Scotsman, in his great remorse, tried to make amends for his violence: he paid for the repair of the wrecked hotel rooms; sent Lillie expensive clothes and jewellery, even gave her the choice of his thoroughbred colts. Lillie remained adamant and refused to have anything more to do with him. Then Baird presented Lillie with a magnificent two hundred and twenty foot yacht – the *White Ladye*, waiting for her inspection at Cherbourg. Lillie's charge against Baird was suddenly dropped. But American reporters who discovered the facts behind this extravagant present, nicknamed the yacht the *Black Eye*.

Lillie in her autobiography simply states that the second horse she owned after her partnership of Flirt with Reggie, 'was a present from an eccentric young bachelor, with vast estates in Scotland, a large breeding stud, a racing-stable, and more money than he knew what to do with.' The two-year-old chestnut colt was called Milford and continued to be trained in Baird's stables. In fact, Lillie confessed, 'I forgot all about him until Messrs. Weatherby wrote requesting me to register my colours, as the colt, with engagements, had been transferred to me, and was due to run in an important race in a week or so. I happened to be wearing a fawn and blue cloak at the moment, and quickly resolved on that combination.' To hide the true identity of Milford's new owner – Lillie had visions of the lads in the gallery shouting down to her on stage for racing tips – she adopted the name of 'Mr. Jersey'. Milford's first win for Mr. Jersey was at Kempton Park, then he went on to win at Ascot and Newmarket, earning Lillie over £8,000 in stakes.

On Baird's death in 1893, Milford was moved to stables in the village of Kentford, near Newmarket. Here Lillie rented Regal Lodge, with the Royal Coat of Arms over the fireplace in one of its five reception rooms, bought several other horses and made friends with 'the most astute racing man of his day' – Captain James Machell. As Lillie recalled: 'He was past his prime when we met, having only recently recovered from a sad mental lapse, but by figuratively sitting at his feet I learned much in a comparatively short time.'

Once Lillie had started owning horses, there was no stopping her. As Bertie, too, was a race horse owner, this made for friendly rivalry between them, as well as a renewal of the bond of affection between them. Soon Lillie had about twenty horses in training and was about to be persuaded to buy another – an Australian horse called Merman – on the advice of Mr. Allinson of the London office of the International Horse Agency. 'When I strolled into Mr. Allinson's office in Pall Mall it was certainly not with the idea of purchase, yet he was so certain he was right this time that in half an hour he had persuaded me to become the owner of the horse, later pronounced by Machell and Sloan to be the best long-distance runner of his time in the world.'

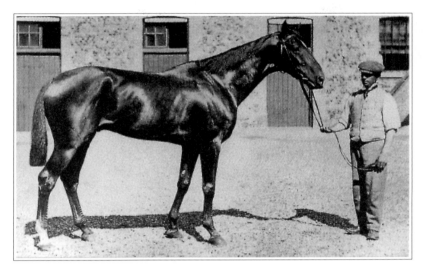

Lillie's horse 'Merman'.

To begin with Merman did not win a single race. Then Lord Beresford suggested the horse might do better running barefoot, as Australian horses usually did on their own race-courses. Lillie acted on his suggestion and immediately Merman started to win. His greatest success came in 1897, the year of Queen Victoria's Diamond Jubilee: he won the Cesarewitch, giving Lillie her largest winnings ever – £120,000. 'The Cesarewitch was the first handicap I appropriated, and although I controlled my feelings and appeared, I hope, outwardly calm, I was really trembling with excitement.' The Prince of Wales himself, defying the rules, pub-licly escorted Lillie into the sacred precincts of the Jockey Club enclosure.

This success added an extra happiness to Lillie's forty-fourth birthday. 'I had people staying with me for the meeting, and others to dinner, and my old chef – who was a bit of an artist –

had a birthday cake already baked, and decorated it in coloured sugar with Merman winning by a neck from The Rush. How prophetic!'

The year 1897, however, had not been such a happy one for Edward Langtry. He was spending more and more of Lillie's monthly allowance on drink and, in that autumn, while crossing from Liverpool to Belfast, he fell down the steamer's companion ladder, sustaining severe injuries to his head and face. On reaching Belfast, Edward was taken to the Royal Infirmary for medical attention. After his release, he decided to return to London, but for some reason got out of the train at Crewe and was twice found wandering on the line in a dazed condition. When a doctor had redressed his head injuries, Edward stayed out all Sunday night and was found in a confused state and with only a few pence in his pocket on the Monday. The Magistrate, to whom he was then taken, straightaway committed him to Upton Mental Asylum. Edward died on Friday, 14th October, just two days after Lillie had won her fortune at Newmarket.

While he was being questioned as to his identity, it was reported in the newspaper that 'he had said that he had been married twenty-five years and that his wife had had a divorce from him and had had to go to the colonies to get it.' Later, Detective Perkins told a reporter on *The Star*: 'Mrs. Langtry passed through to and from Ireland. On every occasion he knew the time she would arrive and was invariably at the station some hours before the train or boat was due. He would walk up and down, growing more and more excited until half an hour before the time of her arrival. Then he would single out a porter and say, 'Boy, I can't stick it any longer. Watch her for me. Look closely at her. Tell me how she looks; does she look well? Is she as beautiful? What she wears. Be careful about her dress and tell me all about it.' Then he would dart out of the station. After the train or boat had gone he would come back and question the porter most minutely, and sob as if his heart would break as he learned the details and walk off the station sobbing, and apparently dazed.'

Edward's funeral was, according to the local paper, 'an extremely quiet one. Dr. Hollis and Mrs. Hollis (Mr. Langtry's sister) were the only relations who attended, the others being Mr. Cornelius Collins with whom the deceased lodged at Southampton and Dr. Renton and Mr. A.B.Hornby representing the Asylum's authorities. Mrs. Langtry sent a beautiful wreath of lilies of the valley, violets, etc., tied with purple ribbon.'

Merman Cottage, Beaumont.

12 Two Marriages in the Family

By 1898, WHEN LILLIE WAS still only forty-five, she had amassed through her theatrical success and shrewd investments a private fortune of more than two million dollars. She had also formally retired from the stage. A year later, Jeanne-Marie, now eighteen, became engaged to Ian Malcolm, high ranking member of the prestigious MacCullum clan, Conservative M.P. for Stowmarket and, at thirty-three, one of the most eligible bachelors in London.

Marriage was in Lillie's mind too. Freddie Gebhard had eventually married someone else; she had finally declined the proposal of the Hungarian born and vastly rich Prince Esterhazy de Golantha, who was verging on sixty. Instead, she agreed to become the wife of the much younger and less rich Hugo Gerald de Bathe. The tall and handsome Hugo, the eldest son of Sir Henry de Bathe, was nineteen years her junior and just seven years older than Jeanne-Marie.

The couple were married in Jersey on 27th July, 1899 in the same church where Lillie had married Edward Langtry, only the Rector this time was not her father but Edward Luce. On the marriage certificate Hugo's status was gentleman and Lillie's was the widow of Edward Langtry; her father was named simply as the Dean of Jersey. That very same day Lillie's horse Merman happened to win her several more thousands of pounds at Goodwood. Interestingly, the Jersey papers carried news of the Goodwood races and their winners, but not a word of Lillie and Hugo's secret wedding. The cottage at Beaumont which Lillie bought to be their Jersey home was, naturally, called 'Merman.'

Jersey life, however, was not to suit Lillie for long. Once the Boer War had begun and Hugo volunteered to join the British forces in South Africa, Lillie was back on stage in London. The theatre was the Haymarket, the play Sydney Grundy's 'The Degenerates' and, because by now the secret of her second marriage had somehow become common knowledge, the play's entire run was sold out before the opening night.

The same box office success was assured when Lillie took 'The Degenerates' to New York, when the *New York Herald Tribune* reported: 'Every seat in the house was occupied from orchestra rail to back bench of the gallery.' It also noted of Lillie herself: 'It was quickly seen that she had not lost a detail of her beauty or personal charm during her long absence. She was in every way the Mrs. Langtry of old, as handsome as ever, as distinguished in bearing – the same wonderfully engaging eyes and smile – as when she had said 'au revoir' to New York a few seasons ago. As an actress she was improved since she was last here.'

It was with this same play that Lillie decided to open the Opera House in Jersey. It had just been built to replace the Theatre Royal which had burned down nearly ten years after her appearance there. *The Jersey Times* gave an ecstatic report of the inaugural performance:

> That the 9th of July will long live in the memory of many is a certainty, for yesterday marked the opening of the new Opera House replacing the old Theatre Royal in Gloucester Street, and such an event is naturally of no small importance in our little community.... Expressions of genuine admiration at the beauty of the interior decorations could be heard on all sides....last evening's was one of the most brilliant and representative house ever present at a first night performance in Jersey.....let us say the whole performance was a veritable triumph, and plainly afforded intense enjoyment. Never, perhaps, has 'The Degenerates' been presented to a more interested audience, for even if a trifle frigid at first, the house soon warmed-up and

followed each and every point with the keenest interest.

At the end of the performance Lillie came on stage to thank the audience for their affectionate welcome and went on to say:

> Ladies and gentlemen and old friends, I thank you most heartily for the welcome you have given me. I am not surprised at it, for Jersey people are very clannish. We do cling. I promised after your old theatre was burnt down to open your new one, and I have performed my promise though it is in the midst of my holidays. As a matter of fact, I should have been jealous had anyone else opened it, for it seemed to me my right to do so. (Loud applause). One never truly misses a thing until it is lost, and you must have missed your old play-house when it was burnt down. But now you have got this really artistic, compact delightful and beautiful new house, I hope you will give it all the support in your power. As a Jersey-woman I cannot do better than conclude with a little Jersey patois, a quotation, in fact, from one of our local poets.

It was her reciting in Jersey Norman-French – no record remains of the exact poem – that gave rise to the most spontaneous outburst of applause.

~

Queen Victoria lived just over a year into the twentieth century. In January, 1901, at the age of eighty-one, she died and the fifty-nine-year-old Bertie finally became King. He immediately appointed Louis Battenberg – now married to Princess Victoria of Hesse – to be his personal aide. That same year, Lillie bought the leasehold of the Imperial Theatre. It was right next to the Royal Aquarium, where she had had that chance meeting in 1876 with Lord Ranelagh which was to change her life. The huge theatre was in a bad state of repair and would need a great deal of money to modernise but, according to Lillie herself, 'I fell more and more in love with bricks and mortar and marble and gold, so that when the beautiful theatre was completed I had spent nearly fifty thousand pounds on its conversion. The marble of different colouring which lined the walls was all especially quarried in Italy, and the colour-scheme of the furnishings, curtains, banners, etc., was that of nature's spring garb – purple, green, and gold....The play that was really the cause of all this expenditure and trouble was called 'The Royal Necklace', and dealt with the episode in which the unfortunate Marie Antoinette, Cardinal Rohan, and Madame de la Motte were concerned, but it was certainly not worthwhile. Spectacular and beautifully mounted and costumed, it yet had the inexcusable fault of dullness, and only ran a few months.' Lillie had no better success with her second play 'Mlle Mars' and at last realised 'that Westminster, although only three minutes from Charing Cross was, and still is, out of the playgoer's beat.'

The Imperial did, however, have one memorable night – 'I had in conjunction with Hartley Manners written a play called 'The Crossways', which I was to tour in the States, and on the eve of my departure, the King, on hearing of our literary effort, commanded a performance. So the theatre was reopened for a single night. The King and Queen occupied the royal box, while the stalls and boxes were filled by their Majesties' friends, the pit and gallery tickets being offered by me to the Queen, who caused them to be distributed among the humbler members of the house-hold servants, and I was told it was amusing to see them wait to take their cue to applaud from the Royals. The play was a success, and I was summoned to the royal room to be congratulated.'

Lillie ruefully summed up the short history of the extravagantly restored Imperial Theatre, which she eventually had to sell at a loss, in the words of an epitaph found on a baby's tomb:

If I was soon done for,
I wonder why I was begun for.

The second marriage in the family took place in 1902 when Jeanne-Marie was married to Ian Malcolm. The ceremony was held in St Margaret's Church, Westminster and she was, unusually, given away not by a male relative but by her mother. As well as the presents of a cheque and a diamond brooch, Lillie settled £5,000 a year on her daughter, while Bertie sent her his best wishes and some jewellery. On the marriage certificate, the name of her father was given as Edward Langtry, deceased. But, in fact, and quite by accident, Jeanne-Marie had learned who her true father was just before her wedding, as her own daughter, Mary Malcolm, explained: 'It seems that shortly before the wedding in June 1902 of Jeanne-Marie and Ian Malcolm, the couple were invited to a society dinner party given by Margot, Lady Asquith. The formidable Lady Asquith asked Jeanne-Marie, who was only 18 [sic], what her father was giving her as a wedding present. 'Oh, but Lady Asquith,' Jeanne replied, 'my father is dead.' Her hostess chuckled. 'Oh, I don't mean him, I mean your real father.' My mother burst into tears and rushed from the room. But the humiliation was worsened when her fiance told her that her mother had already told him that Jeanne's real father was Prince Louis of Battenberg. That, in other words, she was illegitimate.'

Jeanne-Marie's love for her mother had survived Lillie publicly accepting her as her daughter only when she was in her teens; the fact that first Lillie's brother Maurice, who had died in India, and then Edward Langtry had been claimed as her father, but this revelation was too much to bear. She no longer wished to have anything to do with her mother. So when Jeanne-Marie's visits to her stopped, Lillie felt she had to write to her: 'My darling Jeanne ... I think, darling the time has come for some sort of explanation. You have been in town all this week and have never been near me ... Whatever [the reason] is I should like to know, for I feel that I have nothing to reproach myself with ... I think I have always shown my intense love for you, and to be in the same town with you and not see you makes me so wretched that

I am quite ill. Please darling write me a nice letter.'

The reply to her letter came three days later:

My dear mother,

... I feel sure you cannot have forgotten the unhappy incident that occurred on the eve of my marriage, when it became my painful duty to ask you a certain question concerning my parentage. After having been left to ascertain the cruel truth for myself I came to you, my mother, either to confirm or deny it. Alas, I knew the latter to be impossible and was quite prepared for what I was sure would be your answer. Remembering as you must the sympathetic denial I received, can you wonder that from that moment my feelings should have changed completely? That answer, coming from the one person whom all my life I have loved and respected, shattered my ideas and killed all affection in me. What I suffered the last days under your roof, knowing this change to have come upon me yet feeling powerless to alter it ... Had it not been for the support of the pure love and devotion of the strong man who wished to make me his wife, in spite of all, I think I should have gone mad.

... I have felt within the last year or two that our tastes are widely different. Therefore we had best live our own lives apart. In conclusion, please believe that, painful as I know it must be to you to receive this letter, the necessity for writing it causes the most intensive misery to your daughter — Jeanne.

From that time on Jeanne treated her mother almost as she would a complete stranger.

13 Six Months in South Africa

APART FROM THE IRRECONCILABLE BREAK with her daughter and the mistaken purchase of the Imperial Theatre, the first years of the twentieth century went well for Lillie. In 1900 her horse Merman won one of the world's most important races – the Ascot Gold Cup – as well as a great deal of money. She always regretted, though, not having been at Ascot on the actual day, but, as she remembered, 'I was on a visit to my mother in Jersey, and I was so absorbed in landing a shoal of mackerel in St. Aubin's Bay with my old fisherman on the day, that I forgot all about racing momentarily. Late in the afternoon I went into the town of St. Heliers to find my racing-colours flying everywhere, even tied to the whips of the cabbies, while from the office of the local paper rushed the editor shouting like a schoolboy, 'You've won!'

In 1900, too, there had been her rousing welcome at Jersey's Opera House and, two years later, the Command Performance of her co-written play 'Crossways'. Then, in 1904, two years after the end of the Boer War, Lillie became a grandmother on the birth of Jeanne's first child. But despite being a grandmother and now fifty-one, Lillie readily accepted an unexpected invitation from an impressario into the unknown – a tour of South Africa.

Lillie's choice for her company's repertoire on the six months' tour included the already popular 'As You Like It' and 'The Degenerates', plus two new plays, 'Walls of Jericho' and 'Mrs Deering's Divorce'. It is no surprise that Lillie chose the latter, because her performance in America as Mrs. Deering had caused such welcome publicity, with the *New York Times* commenting:

'Mrs. Langtry has made a career of shocking the American theatre-going public, and this time she goes far beyond the bounds of good taste by unnecessarily removing her clothes on stage. She cannot be faulted for wanting to demonstrate that her figure would be the envy of a woman of thirty, but one expects a greater sense of propriety when an actress of Mrs. Langtry's stature steps on stage.' What had Lillie done? She had taken off her gown and revealed herself to the audience in a full-length slip before putting on her dressing wrap.

The tour started in Durban in the spring of 1905 and Lillie remembered, 'There was a great deal of rehearsing to get through before opening in three days, and the following morning I found a rickshaw of my very own waiting outside, with a solemn-looking, hulking Zulu as 'pony', named Jim. The theatre wardrobe-mistress had made him a loin-cloth of my racing colours, turquoise and fawn, and with huge pampas grasses, dyed to match, standing upright on his head, scarlet hibiscus flowers over each ear, and calabashes of snuff and so forth hanging everywhere, he was a 'glowing' sight.'

As well as a public luncheon arranged in Lillie's honour, a race-meeting was also put on specially for her. 'The race-cards were printed in my colours. I was presented with many racing trophies, and I watched most of the racing from the steward's stand – the only woman who had ever invaded the sacred precincts'.

At the end of Lillie's stay in Durban, 'Jim seemed so cut up at leaving me that I thought it would soften his grief if I gave him a souvenir as well as the prosaic tip. I therefore took the giant Zulu to a Curio shop and bade him choose a string of beads or something native that he could add to the extensive collection already adorning his person. But he turned his back on these gewgaws and seized the most valuable bundle of ostrich feathers in the shop. The indignant proprietor snatched them from him and substituted a cheap feather boa. The negro received the humbler present with mitigated joy, but promptly wound it round his woolly head in company with the cattle horns dyed pampas and calabashes.'

Next stop was Johannesburg and after that Pretoria, where 'The theatre was as unattractive as were the rather meagre audiences, for the population was largely composed of Boers, who did not flock to see English companies, just then at all events, and I think a long-bearded Boer, who nightly occupied the stage-box, and sent me fruit in washing-baskets, was probably my only Dutch admirer.' But Lillie did take special note of the wall over which Winston Churchill made his escape, after being taken prisoner in the Boer War. 'I snapshotted it and sent him a copy.' Also in Pretoria Lillie discovered the Zoological Gardens and was not only delighted to make the acquaintance of Dr. Gunning who ran the Gardens, but also to receive from him the present of 'the dearest little meercat' which she immediately called 'Pretoria'.

'By the time we reached the Mount Nelson Hotel at Cape Town, the pretty little African squirrel had realised that she had nothing to fear, and she became quite saucy, playing hide-and-seek about the passages of the hotel, and sitting on my shoulder in a friendly manner. One day, finding a newly-landed hotel arrival's door open, she galloped round and round the room, terrifying the occupant.

She really was the spirit of mischief, tearing the muslin blinds into strips so that she could look out more easily, eating my white shoes, on or off my feet, and burrowing into the springs of the easy chairs to make herself a comfortable resting place, so that only the merest tip of her curled tail could be seen. At sunset exactly she ceased her capers and crept into the darkest corner to sleep, whence even the sound of cracking nuts could not dislodge her.' Among the humans whose company she also enjoyed in Cape Town were Sir Starr Jameson, Premier of the Union of South Africa, and the English writer Rudyard Kipling.

Another of Lillie's passions besides her love of animals was plants, as it had been her mother's. She particularly delighted in the scenery round Cape Town. 'The flora of the Cape was extremely fascinating to an amateur gardener like myself, the mountain being carpeted in parts with spreading masses of the large, wax-like, flowered heather, pink, red, yellow and white, that only endure under glass in England, and look meagre and unhappy at that.....But Cape Colony is a veritable garden of all kinds of floral treasures and, of course, the various amaryllis, belladonnas, nerines, etc., are indigenous, and arum lilies grow in the fields.' In fact, she admitted that Cape Town was the only town during her South African tour that she regretted leaving.

One of the actors on tour with Lillie was Robert Bland and his detailed memories throw an interesting light on her both as a person and as an actress: 'Although she had not lost her beauty at that time, it was not so wondrous as it had been. There was only one woman in South Africa who in any way approached her, and she was in Johannesburg when we arrived in the town. She was an Englishwoman, very beautiful, witty, and many years younger than Mrs. Langtry, who was frankly jealous of her.

Charles Sugden, who was with us, knew this woman, and put a box at her disposal one night when we were playing 'The Walls of Jericho'. After one of his scenes he went into the box in his make-up and sat, as he thought, out of sight, but the proud, steady gaze of Mrs. Langtry alighted upon him, and filled his mind with apprehension. There is a clause in most theatrical contracts forbidding actors to appear in the front of the 'house' in 'make-up.'

Mrs. Langtry sent a message to Sugden requesting him to leave the box. Sugden refused to do so, and without a moment's hesitation, Mrs. Langtry sent for her stage manager and told him to find a substitute for Mr. Sugden for the night's performance. Up to that time no understudy rehearsals had taken place, and Monckton Hoffe (author of the delightful play 'The Little Damozel') was called upon to 'mug' the part, and he sat up all night with towels round his head trying to get the lines. He played the part the next night and gave a very creditable performance. Mrs. Langtry was angry, and she had a will of iron. Poor Sugden was in despair, and he never appeared again under her management. He returned to London and brought a suit against Mrs. Langtry, which was settled later out of court.'

Bland then attempts to describe Lillie, whom he confessed he liked 'immensely'. 'Her neck and shoulders were superb, her legs thin and shapeless. She tried to hide this defect when playing Rosalind in 'As You Like It'. Her light brown hair grew gracefully, and was worn in the nape of the neck. Her skin was lovely, and she owed this, I think, to her magnificent health. She had very beautiful grey-blue eyes, a fine sensitive nose, good teeth, a largish mouth, and well defined lips.'

Though Bland was prepared to concede that Lillie was a great woman, he did not believe that she was a great actress as well. He also thought that Lillie herself was too sensible a person to think of herself as an actress in the first rank. But he did admit, that as Rosalind in 'As You Like It', she gave a very good performance. However, he did have one worry about the play. 'I played Oliver and as she was supposed to faint in my arms in one scene I was always fearful about dropping her. She would never have forgiven me had I done so. Fortunately, with the aid of a good deal of staff work, I managed to evade the dreaded issue. She was seen at her best, I thought, in the play Sydney Grundy wrote for her, 'The Degenerates'. The people of Johannesburg like her so well in this play that we were not called upon to put up anything else.'

Bland's final comments about Lillie were also most complimentary: 'Mrs. Langtry was always well turned out. Nothing untidy about her. When we did a two-days' journey in South Africa some of the women of the company were untidy, and wore peignoirs in the morning. Not so Mrs. Langtry. At eight o'clock she was as any woman to be seen in Bond Street on a May morning.' He summed up the effect of Lillie's South African tour with the words: 'Mrs. Langtry was the first English theatrical 'star' to take a company to South Africa, and on her arrival at Durban on the *Walmer Castle* made some stir. The mayor went aboard to greet her, and a brass band played inappropriate music when she went down the gangway with a large bouquet of flowers in her arms. Unlike most actresses, she hated that sort of thing. It was no note of superiority, but underlying her detestation of the methods of advertising was something fine, bearing on an inherent sincerity in her nature.'

Before her visit to South Africa, Lillie was told that she would feel the call to return but, though she said she had enjoyed her six months tour and gained financially from it, she never did go back. She already had new ventures in mind.

14 New Ventures to the End

WITH TYPICAL ENERGY AND COURAGE, Lillie adapted to the changing mood of the Edwardian period and also faced the rigours of wartime from 1914-18. Being in her fifties, or even sixties, certainly did nothing to dampen her enthusiasm for new ventures during the first two decades of the twentieth century. As had happened throughout her life, some of these ventures brought her further into the limelight, others lost her a great deal of money.

After her physically exhausting South African tour, Lillie relaxed back in England at Regal Lodge with a particularly successful summer season at the races. In the autumn, though, came the moment for her to decide in which direction her career should now go. With her usual shrewdness and Jersey eye for a good bargain, Lillie decided to turn her back on the theatre proper and start up in the world of vaudeville, where the increasingly high financial rewards were more attractive.

So it was, that twelve days before her fifty-third birthday, Lillie made her first appearance in vaudeville. The date was 1st October 1906, the place the Fifth Avenue Hotel in New York. Lillie's part in the twenty minute melodrama, with the enigmatic title 'Between the Daytime and the Night', was as the faithless wife who is finally shot by her husband and dies dramatically centre stage. She later appeared in both British as well as American vaudeville in a shortened version of the popular 'The Degenerates' under its new title 'The Right Sort'. No wonder that she was considered one of the most hard-working actresses of her day.

It was about this time that Lillie was credited with starting a particular theatrical tradition. She apparently asked the manager of the theatre where she was playing if he would be so good as to lay a carpet from her dressing room to the stage. Its purpose? To keep the hems of her dresses from getting dirty. The manager laid down the carpet, which happened to be red, but before he knew where he was, all the other actresses were clamouring for their bit of red carpet too. So it seems that a chance request by Lillie was the origin of the now well-known phrase – 'Roll out the red carpet'.

In between her vaudeville appearances, Lillie liked to go to Paris for new clothes; spend as much of the summer as she could at the races; and, once she had discovered the delights of Monte Carlo, while away the winter months gambling. Here, too, she would often meet Bertie, hiding behind the pseudonym of Baron Renshaw. Unfortunately, her luck on the race-course did not, to begin with, extend to the gaming tables and Lillie soon found she was losing at the casinos almost as much as she was earning. 1907, however, proved to be a turning point in her fortunes in more ways than one. First of all Lillie became the first woman to break the bank at Monte Carlo; secondly, because of the death that same year of her father-in-law, Sir Henry de Bathe, she now had the pleasure of signing herself Lady de Bathe.

There was, however, one former interest that Lillie decided to relinquish. Though in 1908 yet another of the horses she had bought – this time Yentoi, under the management of her new trainer Fred Darling – had won the Cesarewitch, she had no success at all in breeding winners. So despite having had high hopes of her stud farm at Gazely, near Newmarket, she gradually realised it would be best to close down such an expensive and unprofitable enterprise.

Almost immediately though, that interest was replaced by another – Lillie wanted to try her hand as a novelist. The tale she had to tell was peopled by typical Edwardian society: there was the 'charming and most insouciante of widows', Louisa

Lady de Bathe on the cover of The Bystander, *April, 1908.*

Renshaw; her fiancée, the South American millionaire Ernest Gattlinger; and her titled friends Lady Minnie Vernham and Lord Kit Vernham – 'a typical Englishman, kind-hearted, good-natured, easy going, a thorough sportsman, a most devoted husband.' Was it a coincidence that Louisa should share the same surname with one of Bertie's aliases, Baron Renshaw?

The plot hinges on a practical joke thought up by Louisa. This is that Minnie should sail to America in Louisa's place, calling herself Mrs. Renshaw. On the same ship will be Minnie's husband Kit, crossing the Atlantic on doctor's orders for the sake of his health. Louisa likes the idea and thinks that, as her husband could be beginning to take her 'as a matter of course,' it might be 'a useful lesson to him to see her surrounded by admiring gallants.' So a trail of misunderstanding aboard the *Kaiser Fritz* is set – with nice details observed from Lillie's own experience of transatlantic crossings – and in twenty-eight amusing chapters and in her own direct style of narration, Lillie manages to untangle the mistaken identities and bring all her characters to a happy ending. The novel, in keeping with its light-hearted mood, was given the punning title *All at Sea*; was finely illustrated by the well-known illustrator Henry Brock; and published in 1909 by Hutchinson. It brought her in royalties of £1,200 and was reviewed as witty, clever and bright, but also, as one critic said, too full of stupid epigrams.

In real life, the following May, Lillie's royal lover Bertie, now sixty-nine, had a severe attack of bronchitis. While assuring those around his sick-bed 'I shall go on,' the king's health rapidly deteriorated; he fell into a coma and on 6th May he died. In his will he had ordered that all his private and personal papers, even letters from his wife, be destroyed. This wish obviously included all those letters he had received over the years from his 'Chère Amie', Lillie Langtry. As the coffin of AE – his signature on his letters to her – was taken through the streets of London on its way to Windsor Castle, his favourite cousin, Louis Battenberg, marched alongside the gun-carriage on which it rested. Lillie watched the funeral procession from her private balcony in the Berkeley Hotel.

For the summer months after Bertie's death, Lillie lived quietly, but in the autumn and for the next three years she was back to playing in the vaudeville circuit on both sides of the Atlantic. But in 1913 Lillie had her sixtieth birthday and was eager for her next venture – the world of films. The Hungarian film producer Adolphe Zukor had taken his Famous Players Company into this new form of entertainment that same year and one of the first films he made, shot in two top-floor studios in New York, was the comedy-drama 'His Neighbour's Wife'. Lillie was included in the cast because Zukor strongly believed, 'The public wants to see the great Lillie Langtry'.

When the silent film opened on 14th October in New York's Lyric Cinema, one review commented, 'The Jersey Lily was a fine-figured woman, magnificently gowned, languid and dramatic, of horrified glances and rather too sweet forgiving smiles.' A screen still, showing Lillie about to save her husband from being shot by the husband of the woman he happened to be passionately kissing, explains the 'horrified glances'. Zukor in later years remembered, 'Much of her beauty remained, though her straight but full features might now have better been described as handsome.' But Lillie was not as photogenic as she had been paintable and the financial rewards at that time were not great, so she made no other film appearances.

During the Great War, when Hugo, Clement and Ian Malcolm joined up and Louis Battenberg was forced to change his German name to Mountbatten, Lillie showed both bravery and generosity, as well as using her undoubted organising ability to boost morale and help the war-effort. She chose to produce Sidney Grundy's latest play 'Mrs. Thompson', and put it on first in London's Drury Lane, advertising in the daily papers that she would donate her own salary and any profit to the Red Cross. She did the same when she took the play to New York. She also gave benefit performances for the troops on both sides of the Atlantic.

On one of these trips from Liverpool to New York, in 1916, Lillie, now sixty-three, met the writer Somerset Maugham. His memories of that meeting were published in 1949 in his *Writers' Notebook* and make interesting reading:

Mrs. Langtry was on board. We neither of us knew anybody so we spent much of our time together. I had never known her well before. She still had a fine figure and a noble carriage, and if you were walking behind her you might have taken her for a young woman. She told me she was sixty-six. Her eyes, which they say were so beautiful, were much smaller than one would have expected, and their blue, once intense, I believe, was pale. The only remains of her beauty were her short upper lip and her engaging smile. She used very little make-up. Her manner was easy, unaffected and well-bred; it was that of a woman of the world who had always lived in good society.

She made one remark which I think is the proudest thing I ever heard a woman say. The name of Freddy Gebhardt recurred frequently in her conversation one day and I, to whom it was new, at last asked who he was.

'You mean to say you've never heard of Freddy Gebhardt?' she cried with real astonishment. 'Why, he is the most celebrated man in two hemispheres.'

'Why?' I enquired.

'Because I loved him,' she answered.

She told me that during her first season in London she had only two evening dresses, and one of these was a day dress which by the pulling out of a string could be arranged for wearing at night. She told me that in those days no woman made up, and her advantage was the brilliant colouring that she had by nature. The excitement she caused was so intense that when she went to the livery stable to mount her hired horse to ride in the park they had to shut the gates to keep out the crowd.

She told me that she had been very much in love with the Crown Prince Rudolf and he had given her a magnificent emerald ring. One evening they had a quarrel, and in the course of it she snatched his ring off her finger and threw it in the fire. With a cry he flung himself down on his knees and scrabbled out (this was the word she used) the burning coals to save the valuable stone. Her short upper lip curled scornfully as she related the incident. 'I couldn't love him after that,' she said.

I saw her two or three times after we arrived in New York. She was mad about dancing and went nearly every night to a dance hall. She said the men danced beautifully and you only had to pay them fifty cents. It gave me a nasty turn to hear her say this so blandly. The notion of this woman who had had the world at her feet paying a man half a dollar to dance with her filled me with shame.

On her return to England, she had two quite different wartime experiences – one in London and the other in the country – but she described both in the same understated manner, only conveying her natural excitement on the news that the war was at last over. 'Once safely back in England, I played at the Coliseum for a time, and was on the stage at the moment that a bomb demolished John Bull's office. The crowded audience felt it was uncomfortably close, and the gallery made such a din that not a word of the play could be heard. We went on steadily with our lines, and I was surprised to receive an ovation from the audience at the close. Subsequently the stage manager, waiting in the wings, seized my hands and thanked me for my sangfroid, which he said had averted a panic. But as the stage of the theatre with its glass roof was the real danger-spot, the auditorium being protected with sand-bags, I do not know why the packed gallery made such a fuss.'

Soon after this Zeppelin bombing of London, Lillie decided to retire from the stage altogether and go to live in Regal Lodge, where she soon found a friend in the young Louis d'Albani, son of the solicitor who looked after her Newmarket House and other interests. Here she also spent the last year of the war 'cultivating vegetables, with the help of the village girls at Kentford, until the Armistice brought us back to life again. Never shall I forget the village blacksmith running into the stable-yard shouting, 'War -r-r- is over !' in his best Suffolk, and my tempestuous rush to London to join in the celebration. After a world-shaking cataclysm such as we had just been through, ideas and plans which before had seemed of such paramount importance now appeared small and trivial by comparison, and for the time being I found my interest in both acting and racing lapse. I felt weary of the responsibility of owning houses, and was glad enough, when I found eager purchasers to pass mine on to others.'

But this weariness of the responsibility of owning houses was not to last. No sooner had Lillie taken herself, three months later, to the South of France and found herself drifting to her favourite Monaco, than she was house-hunting again. 'I was accompanied in my strenuous search by an indefatigable house-agent , who, after showing me over all sorts of luxurious but conventional villas, pointed out to me, half-way down the ravine of Ste Dévote, a bungalow belonging to one of his croupier friends, which, on account of its unique position, I immediately annexed.'

Typically, as with all her former homes, Lillie was not content until she had made her own personal mark on the property. 'Where there is a will there is a way, even in house construction. I scooped wine-cellars out of rocks, kitchens out of rubble-heaps, and, coaxing a side of the ravine from the Monégasque Government, I made of it one of the most picturesque gardens in the principality. My little house, clinging to a rock, is ideally situated betwixt mountain and sea, and it is impossible for one who loves Nature to be other than happy in such surroundings. My hanging gardens I tend myself – as far as they need gardening, for the inaccessible part of the precipitous rocks clothe themselves with lovely alpines, stocks, maidenhair ferns, wild orchids, wallflowers, bluebells, snapdragons, masses of geraniums, and other unbidden but welcome guests, and even cinerarias perch themselves on lofty ledges, and do better there

Lillie Langtry's villa 'Le Lys' in Monaco.

in their wildness. In the cultivated portion irises, mimosas, daturas, cyclamen, primulas, and all the lovely winter blooming flora thrive.'

Lillie lived in this idyllically placed villa, which she called 'Le Lys' (The Lily) until her death, ten years later. She had living with her, her butler's widow, Matilda Peat, whose devoted service she so much appreciated, and five servants; her husband Hugo she installed in Nice, just half an hour's car drive away, ready to be called upon when the occasion demanded an escort.

It was here in the seclusion of 'Le Lys' that Lillie received both good and bad tidings: in 1920 that Millais' 'A Jersey Lily' had been judged the Royal Academy's Picture of the Year for the third time; in 1921 that her other royal lover and father of her child, Prince Louis, had died; in 1927 that her last remaining brother Clement – who had so often brought his experience as a lawyer to the business deals she made – had died in London. The letter she wrote in reply to the condolences of Seymour Hicks and his wife Ellaline Terris shows how deeply she felt this loss:

Thank you dearest Seymour – I am trying to be brave – your letter helps me and you and dearest Ella showed me how you loved the dear – and suffered also – I want to see – you both before I go. Perhaps Friday afternoon I might come – You were both so good to me today. Clem was so much to me – love to you both.

Lillie de B.

It was here, in Monte Carlo, that she also wrote her recollections – of her childhood in Jersey, her life in London, her stage career and all her many enterprises – which she called *The Days I Knew*. In this autobiography Lillie gives away no secrets, makes no scandalous disclosures, just as she had avoided doing when the Hurst newspapers asked her to write her life-story for them in 1917. Indeed, at the end of *The Days I Knew*, Lillie gently rebukes the reader who wants to know more: 'It must be borne in mind that I have dealt with the late Victorian and Edwardian period, so that they may appear mild to some who are looking for sensation. The fact is that what was considered risqué and compromising then would pass unnoticed in the present day.' Nevertheless, for some people, as much can be learned about Lillie by what she leaves out, as by what she includes.

In the same year that Clement died, for the only time in her life, Lillie disobeyed Gladstone's advice 'never rush into print to explain or defend yourself', but her urgent telegram was actually written to defend Gladstone's own reputation. The case of the 'Slanderous Accusation' was summarised in the *Evening Post*, when it was giving a brief outline of Lillie's life on the day that news of her death reached Jersey:

> In a cause célèbre of 1927 – Capt. Peter Wright's libel action against Viscount Gladstone – allegations were made of a liaison between the great statesman and Lily Langtry. Telegraphing from Nice, where she had a villa, she indignantly repudiated 'the slanderous accusation' and her telegram was read in Court. She treated the matter with characteristic spirit. 'In the olden days this question would have been settled with a horsewhip in the Haymarket,' she said. 'Today things are washed in a Court of Law.'

Whenever Lillie could bring herself to leave her Monégasque paradise, she would travel to London for a short visit. It was on one of these occasions that Lillie had the unexpected pleasure of meeting her youngest grandchild, Mary Malcolm, for the first and only time. Mary told the story of their meeting in her interview with Douglas Keay in 1978: 'I was taken by the governess from our house in Onslow Square to the Cadogan Hotel where Lillie always stayed when she was in London. By this time Lillie was an old lady of 74, plump and cosy with greying fair hair, but still erect. I remember particularly she had lovely legs and feet. I seem to recall she was wearing a shift dress with a very low waistline – all the fashion then – and wore a band round her forehead.

She asked me if I'd like to look in her wardrobe and try on one of her dresses. Then she asked me what I wanted for my birthday, which was still a few months off. I remember my one desire was a Rudge-Whitworth bicycle – the Rolls Royce of bicycles in the 1920s – so I told Lillie. 'Well,' she said, 'that might be a very good idea mightn't it?', but committed herself no further.

It was some weeks later that I arrived home from school to find a large Harrods' van parked outside the front door. Two men in green Harrods' uniform informed me that Lady de Bathe had sent some bicycles for me to chose from.

I never saw Lillie again, and I cannot remember my mother even enquiring about what happened on my only visit to her house.'

Lillie's two eldest grandsons, however, were both allowed to visit 'Le Lys', often staying with their grandmother for a month or more.

~

There were two people in London, though, who were always certain to make Lillie welcome – Bertie's youngest son, now George V, and his wife Queen Mary. In fact, in 1928, the last time that Lillie took tea at Buckingham Palace, King George told her not to hide herself away in Monaco for such long periods, because he for one wanted her to come to London more often.

That autumn, when Lillie celebrated her seventy-fifth birthday, she contracted bronchitis which developed into pleurisy. She was still weak from the effect of this long illness, when early in 1929 she contracted influenza. She died on 12th February and her companion Mrs. Peat, with the tears running down her cheeks, told the correspondent of the *Evening Post* the story of her end:

Yes, it is true; it is true. She has gone. She is dead. I can hardly believe it. The beauty that has returned to her face in death is wonderful. It recalls wonderful associations that this great lady had. Oh, I am tired. I had watched her through the night as her strength ebbed. Dr. Mitchell and the other doctors came in the early hours, and the first light was coming in the Eastern sky when she breathed her last. I cannot realise that never again shall I hear that voice. We did not tell everybody she was so ill, and I did not like to believe her when she kept telling me during the past three days that she thought she was going to die. 'I am going, my dear. I am going to die,' she told me on Sunday morning. She had been in bed for the past three weeks, but her courage was undimmed until Sunday. All day yesterday she turned to me and with a voice growing weaker and weaker, kept declaring that she was 'going.' Twice she said 'Goodbye,' and in fact that was the last word I heard from her lips.

The very first telegram of condolence that Lillie's family received came from George V and Queen Mary.

15 Lillie's Last Wishes

ONE OF LILLIE'S LAST WISHES was that she should not be cremated, but that her body should be taken back to Jersey and buried at St. Saviour's Church where she had worshipped as a young girl, close to the Sunday School she had regularly attended and to the Rectory where she was born. Her body was brought back to Jersey from St. Malo on 22nd February and lay in state in the church overnight, next to a marble urn containing the ashes of her brother Clement, which had been specially sent over from London to be buried in their parents' grave.

The *Evening Post* of Saturday, 23rd February, records details of the funeral the following day:

> Early this afternoon folk began to wend their way up St. Saviour's Hill to the fine old Norman church, and before the hour at which the service had been fixed several hundred people had congregated outside, the doors not being opened until the mourners had arrived.
>
> The funeral service commenced at 3.30, and apart from being fully choral, was simple in nature. As the mourners assembled, the organist (Mr. Cecil Hotton) played appropriate music. The service itself was conducted by the Very Rev. S. Falle, M.A. (Dean), assisted by the Rev. G.P. Balleine, Rector. Psalm 90 was chanted, and the deceased's two favourite hymns, 'Hark, hark my soul,' and 'There is a Blessed Home', were very feelingly sung.

Among the mourners were Lillie's daughter, now Lady Malcolm; her eldest grandson, George Malcolm; Mrs. Peat and Mr. Ommanay, her London solicitor and executor; together with the Bailiff of Jersey and other Island dignitaries. Among the floral tributes were those sent by Lillie's cousin Francis Thorne of St. Aubin; Lt. Col. Le Breton; Lady Florence Boot; the Directors of Luce's Eau de Cologne; the Jersey Green Room Club and several society names in Monaco. Her husband Hugo de Bathe was neither among the mourners, nor did he send any flowers from Nice. There is no record either that Arthur Jones was present at Lillie's funeral.

Lillie's funeral at St. Saviour's Church, Jersey.

Lillie had changed her will only three months before she died, after being so ill in London the previous autumn. Now, in her final wishes for the distribution of all the fine items she had inherited, been given, or bought herself, the first specific legacy in her will was to the Islanders of Jersey. To the Museum in Pier Road, St. Helier, she gave some of her fashionable furniture from Villa Le Lys, including her dining room suite; her drawing room set of Louis XVI fauteuils and settee and mantle clock; her bed, Brittany ward-robe, her gilt and turquoise toilet service, her silver gilt mirror, all her coloured glass and her Viennese dinner service. She also gave, as well as some of the costume jewellery she had worn as Cleopatra, the portrait Sir Edward Poynter had painted of her. She added that should the Museum be unwilling to accept all or any of the items, they were then to go to Mathilda Peat.

When it came to bequests for her immediate family, Lillie bequeathed to her daughter all the rest of her silver and her mother-of-pearl dessert service; to three of her grandchildren she gave £5,000, but only £1,000 to the eldest George, because 'he would be amply provided for on the death of his parents.' Individually she also gave George the silver épergne she had inherited from her great-uncle, Sir Thomas Le Breton; to Victor the Jockey Club Cup Merman had won; to Angus a Georgian tray inherited from her father; and to Mary her diamond, pearl and emerald clock.

To her companion and friend Mathilda Peat, 'as a token of affection and gratitude,' she gave £10,000, all her clothes, furs and jewellery, the Sheffield plate tea-set that she had used daily, her car, the Villa Le Lys, together with all its contents that had not been bequeathed elsewhere. To her solicitor's son, Louis d'Albani – 'late Major in the First 123rd Rifles' – she left a legacy of two thousand pounds. To all her servants at Le Lys who had been with her for more than six months, she left a year's wages. To her husband Hugo, to whom she had always given all he required in Nice, she bequeathed nothing.

Mathilda Peat, in 'Hommage Reconnaissant', commissioned J. Galle of Nice to make a bust of Lillie to stand outside the church in the Clos de l'Hôtel Dieu. It was to be in white marble, with a miniature figure in mourning on her right and a Jersey lily on her left. It was to be placed in front of the marble cross that marked the grave of Lillie's parents and her two brothers Reggie and Clement, so that Lillie could forever look towards the Rectory, now known as 'La Belle Maison', where she was born. Jeanne, as she now preferred to be called, wanted a large tablet to be put on the north wall of the Lady Chapel in memory of her mother. But St. Saviour's Church authorities were not keen on having such a large memorial to a former parishioner with such a questionable reputation and Jeanne was persuaded to put up a tablet a third of the original size she had planned.

So it was that, with the death of one whom many regarded as the best known person of her time, the *New York Tribune* felt it was no exaggeration to proclaim 'An Era has come to an end.' While the unidentified H.L., in the *Evening Post* carrying the story of Lillie's death, expressed many Islanders' bereft feelings more lyrically in the words:

> *Farewell, our Island's fairest flower.*
> *A sad farewell from all your friends –*
> *Both old and young – and rich and poor,*
> *Who love you till all memory ends,*
> > *Dear Lily of Jersey.*
> > > *At Rest*

> *Beauty and talent held the world at your feet,*
> *And though the earth was yours to roam,*
> *Jersey will treasure this memory sweet,*
> *That your thoughts remained with your Island home.*
> > *Dear Lily of Jersey.*
> > > *At Peace.*

Postscript

About Lillie's extraordinary beauty there has never been any doubt, but there has been surprise that she also had a lively mind. She has inspired admiration for daring to be different; but she has also been judged as nothing more than a self-seeking whore. She has been claimed as a feminist; but in 1912 she was the heroine in a play parodying suffragettes.

She was kind when she gave Oscar Wilde money in his last years of exile; but cruel when, as a joke, she fooled the septuagenarian Lord Malmesbury into burning his mouth with unbearably hot food. She was simple enough to be extremely proud of winning a prize in 1924 for the best garden on the Riviera; but sophisticated enough to be one of the first women to smoke in public and be a leader of fashion for most of her life.

Of herself Lillie said, 'I have always been willing to take the blame for things I have done, but it is hard to have blame fastened on me for things I never did.' Looking back on her varied luck she admitted, 'Born in the sign of Libra, the scale has tipped both ways for me'; looking back on her life – though people may on the whole have failed to give her the permanent happiness she sought – she was able to say, 'I have had all that I really wanted very much – a yacht, a racing stable, a theatre of my own, lovely gardens.'

But if Lillie had not been so beautiful could she have achieved so much? She almost lost that beauty once: 'When I was about eleven years old my father brought home, as a novelty, a small spirit stove, which proved so interesting to me that I insisted on cooking some little delicacy over its flame. I wore my hair hanging loose about my shoulders, and in a moment it had caught fire; I ran to my mother in terror, and, in spite of her fright, she succeeded in extinguishing the blaze. My face and neck were horribly burned, but owing to the wonderful nursing and care I received, not the slightest scar was left.'

So the poet Richard Le Gallienne was able after all, to add to the end of *The Days I Knew* the lines:

~ The Jersey Lily ~

All I can bring —
The one gift worthy of you —
Is to bring back again
The wonder and the joy and the delight
Of mortal eyes that saw a little while
The loveliness immortal.

Select Bibliography

Lillie Langtry: *The Days I Knew*, 1925.
Elinor Glyn: *Romantic Adventure*, 1936.
R.H.Bland: *Actor Soldier Poet*, 1939.
G.R.Balleine: *A Bibliographical Dictionary of Jersey*, 1948.
Somerset Maugham: *A Writer's Notebook*, 1949.
E.Dudley: *The Gilded Lily*, 1959.
N.B.Gerson: *Lillie Langtry*, 1971.
H.T.Porter: *Lillie Langtry*, 1973.
J.Brough: *The Prince and the Lily*, 1975.
Birkett & Richardson: *Lillie Langtry*, 1979.
Sheridan Morley: *The Great Stars (Lillie Langtry)*, 1986.
R. Ellman: *Oscar Wilde*, 1987.
T.Aronson: *The King in Love*, 1988.

Newspapers, etc.

British Press and Jersey Times; Evening Post; Jersey Evening Post;
Woman's Own: Sept 30th, 1978.